ERRATUI

1) The caption on page 102 sh(
lows, Tony Doyle in the yellow j(
1984 stage race.

2) The photographs on pages 144-145 should be
reversed.

Tony Doyle: six-day rider

Danny Clark and Tony Doyle, the most successful team on the winter tracks

Tony Doyle:
six-day rider

Geoffrey
Nicholson

Springfield Books Limited

© Geoffrey Nicholson

First published 1992 by Springfield Books Limited, Norman Road, Denby Dale, Huddersfield HD8 8TH, West Yorkshire, England

First edition 1992

British Library Cataloguing in Publication Data

Nicholson, Geoffrey
  Tony Doyle: six-day rider
  I Title
  796.6

ISBN 0 947655 36 0

Photo credits

The author and publishers are grateful to the following for kind permission to reproduce copyright material:

Photosport International for the photos on the half title page and on pages 8, 14, 13 (bottom), 38 (top), 62 (top), 79 (bottom), 85, 96, 106, 115, 119, 124 (bottom), 136, 141 (top), 171
FotoPersBuroWiddershoven for the frontispiece
Graham Watson for the photos on pages 13 (top), 34, 41, 51 (top), 52 (bottom), 62 (bottom), 68, 86, 103, 104, 118 (top), 123, 124 (top), 136, 142, 144, 159
H Roth for the photos on pages 52 (top), 59, 79 (top), 105, 160, 168
Radsport Photos for the photo on page 20
Walter Kraus for the photo on page 22
Rudolph Brauner for the photo on page 33
Detler Konnerth for the photo on page 42
Karl Frank for the photo on page 51 (bottom)
Dan Thisdell for the photo on page 70
Frank Tewksbury for the photo on page 73
Len Thorpe for the photo on page 83
Paul Wright for the photo on page 118 (bottom)
Presse Sports for the photos on pages 141 (bottom), 145
Ronny Meyers for the photo on page 146

Design: Chris Hand, Design for Print
Typesetting: Selwood Systems, Midsomer Norton, Avon
Printed and bound in Hong Kong by Colorcraft Limited

Acknowledgements

In preparing this book I referred to *Cycling Weekly, The European, VeloNews,* and *Velo,* the Belgian yearbook compiled by Harry Van Den Bremt and René Jacobs.

I would also like to thank Ron Webb, Alf Whiteway, Alan Rushton, Mick Bennett, Pierrot De Wit, Paul Wingrave and the Doyle family for their help with background information. And not least, of course, Tony Doyle.

Contents

Chapter 1
The thrill of the chase 9
A winter's tale 1: Dortmund 6 18

Chapter 2
Crash! 23
A winter's tale 2: Grenoble 6 38

Chapter 3
Cruel and unusual punishment 43
A winter's tale 3: Munich 6
and Vienna 3 56

Chapter 4
Anthony Adverse 60
A winter's tale 4: Ghent 6 71

Chapter 5
Wheels of chance 74
A winter's tale 5: Zurich 6 80

Chapter 6
Alf Whiteway of the Clarence 82
A winter's tale 6: Moscow 6 93

Chapter 7
Trial runs 97
A winter's tale 7: Cologne 6 111

Chapter 8
Moscow: retreat to victory 114
A winter's tale 8: Bremen 6 132

Chapter 9
Hard days at the oval office 135
A winter's tale 9: Stuttgart 6 152

Chapter 10
Crock of gold 155
A winter's tale 10: Antwerp 6 172

Chapter 11
The right and wrong side of the tracks 175

Personal records 188
Glossary 190
Bibliography 192

Chapter 1

The thrill of the chase

Early on, because the six-day cycle race chased its own tail round a small indoor track for 144 hours, ending exactly where it had begun, some sports writer called it 'the race to nowhere'. His name was instantly forgotten; the title stuck. Yet it was only part of the truth. Many riders who take up the sport know exactly where they are going. They accept the monotony and danger of the long, hard slog because they know that if they are successful, it will bring them a certain fame and a smallish fortune. But not only that. As boys, they had found out that bikes weren't just for running errands and going on trips. They had become racing cyclists, discovering the thrill of the chase. And in the madison relay, when the two-man teams sling each other in and out of the fray on a rush-hour track at 30 miles an hour and more, the Six provided the most exhilarating chase of all. For some, this excitement eventually becomes blunted by nightly repetition. For others it is constantly renewed, and Tony Doyle, Anthony to his family, is one of these.

From the age of 14, a year after an uncle gave him his first real bike, he seemed to know that cycle racing – and not his previous passion, football – was to be his game. Within a couple of years he had narrowed down his special interest to track racing, although the road still had its attractions. And the fact that London then staged its own six-day race each year, the Skol at Wembley Arena, which he used to go and watch as a schoolboy, focused his ambitions even more sharply.

After, though not as a result of, disappointments at the 1980 Moscow Olympics, he turned professional at 22, with two complementary aims in his career: to win the world professional pursuit title in the summer and to establish himself on the six-day tracks in winter. He has brought off both. He has taken the world title twice, and – something no other British rider

Doyle on the way to winning his first world pro pursuit title at Besançon in 1980

has come within shouting distance of achieving – won 23 Sixes. This makes him the second most successful rider currently on the circuit, behind the Australian, Danny Clark, with whom he shares an all-time record-equalling partnership.

It is a dangerous, arduous, often frustrating career pursued in an artificially lighted cavern cut off from the outside world, and in an atmosphere full of cigar and cigarette smoke, the smell of chips and fried onions, the din of disco music. When the chase is on, and a rider is being constantly buzzed by the rest of the bikes on the track, it's like putting your head in a bees' nest for a living. And this battering of the senses stretches on into the night, with no home comforts at the end of it.

Apart from the risk of accident there is the literal wear and tear of hours in the saddle, the centrifugal force of half a ton which is exerted as the rider comes out of the banking and into the bend, making the tops of the legs ache and often splitting open the skin of scrotum and crutch. The back-to-back scheduling of events, especially in the opening months of the season, means that any short intervals are spent travelling. 'When you go home at the end of the season, you can't sleep at night and you can't wake up in the morning,' Patrick Sercu, winner of a record 88 Sixes, once explained to me. 'It's very bad – takes weeks to get back to a normal life.'

And normal life is what Doyle enjoys. He is a family man; he hurries home; he likes to go into the country on his bike and get rid of the smoke from his lungs. And yet he seems as fascinated by the twilight world of the Sixes as he ever was. He complains about this and that – *this* being generally the injustice of having his riding partner selected by the promoter, not by himself (with a free choice it would always be Clark); *that* being the needlessly squalid living and working conditions off the track. But these things don't ruin the Sixes for him. Now 34, he sees himself riding the boards for another five or six years, as Clark has done, and gives every indication of looking forward to them.

Doyle is 6ft 1in, fair-skinned and strongly built, though he has suffered from back trouble. He is the fourth of five children of an Anglo-Irish family, more noticeably Anglo except for their Catholicism. At 21 Tony married Anne D'Rozario, a warm and friendly but reticent fellow-Catholic whom he had known since his school days and who shared a similarly close-knit, middle-class family background. Her father was an accountant, her mother a nurse from whom she seems to have inherited her placid, capable disposition: 'I'm the calm type. I don't get too anxious or dwell on things.' She is much admired by Doyle's family for the strength she showed after his critical racing accident at Munich in 1989.

At 16, and straight from school, Anne trained as a dispensing optician, a job which helped support them both before Doyle began earning money as a professional rider, and which now she has tailored to suit his comings

10

and goings. Until four years ago she managed the practices in which she worked, but after being unable to get time off one Christmas to join Tony on a trip to Australia, she decided to turn freelance. She is never short of work, and the flexibility suits her. So does her way of life. She has girl friends and her three sisters for company when Tony is away, and even when he retires from racing she would never expect him to take a nine-to-five job. 'We are happy as we are. I'm used to it.'

They now live near Guildford, Surrey, on a green and spacious executive estate of double-fronted neo-Georgian houses reached by short, curving drives in open front gardens. All that distinguishes their house from their neighbours' is that bicycles have priority in the double garage, and the car in the drive bears the name of Doyle's sponsor, latterly *The European*, on its side.

The house is comfortable and beautifully kept inside, but although Doyle's main concerns are represented by the odd framed photograph and poster, there is very little evidence of outside interests. No cat or dog; no bird table in the garden, which is neatly but not ardently kept in various shades of green; no newspapers, except for his sponsor's; no books, although Doyle is famous as a constant reader during lulls in the Sixes; nothing relating to any hobby. No material clues to any other side of his life – in fact no character references at all.

Doyle is not an immediately accessible man. Perhaps it is perverse to say this of someone who has a thoroughly pleasant manner, is generous with his time and attentions, and talks nineteen to the dozen. It's just that often when you look at your notes or play back the tape recorder, he has said less than you thought he had. There is still a certain reserve that you've failed to penetrate.

His mother, Agnes, a very direct person, says that although he sometimes flares up he never bears resentment. She mentions his first meeting with Marat Ganeev after his crash at Munich, which the Soviet rider, by his own admission, had caused. Doyle walked up to him and went as if to hit him, and then put out his arm and shook his hand. She felt she could never have done that herself. But that was Tony, a man who would always prefer to make a joke of things, even though you sometimes feel that he also uses jocularity to cover his traces.

I am not sure about the resentment, but he is certainly slow to apportion blame when things go wrong, especially among friends. He would prefer to think that everything was meant for the best. The word he likes to use to describe his attitude is 'philosophical', and most of the critical remarks he makes take the form of mild sarcasm. 'I expect you have noticed that,' he once remarked. 'I don't suppose you've come across many bike riders as sarcastic as I am, have you?' He asked it with a trace of pride.

11

Doyle has taken a lot of knocks in his career, physical and moral, and perhaps his sarcasm and his jokiness are a necessary armour. 'You notice how diplomatic I am being,' he may say, when what you are hoping for is a bit of red-blooded ruthlessness. But that is not his style. 'We named Tony the ambassador for our sport,' says Alf Whiteway, the founder of Clarence Wheelers and Doyle's great mentor in his early racing days. And sometimes Doyle appears to interpret that as being its press officer.

Alan Rushton, chief executive of Sport for Television, who has been variously Doyle's agent, manager and general adviser since the early 1980s, says:

He's a dream to work with. He is his own walking PR man. He doesn't need PR support. He puts himself over well. Leave him alone with a client, and when you come back he'll have sold them more than you had in the first place. He knows what makes a story – even if sometimes he knows too much what makes a story. It's an unwritten thing that when he decides to pack it in, if he's looking for a job we will definitely have one for him.

His skill as a self-publicist is also vouched for by Martin Ayres, now with Sport for Television but previously editor of *Cycling Weekly*, the sport's main grapevine. It was uncanny, he said, how almost every Sunday night in winter, just as the paper was going to press, Doyle would somehow find a telephone during a break in the Six and ring through with his news. He kept tighter deadlines than most journalists. And unlike other cyclists who rang up from time to time with stories, Doyle was astute enough to give the whole picture – the current laps and points of the first half dozen teams, and their spellings, the main incidents in the race so far. The fact that he would loom large in the report was almost incidental. It was a thoroughly professional performance.

Doyle has always been more than willing to spend his own money to promote his career. In the autumn of 1991, for instance, he took advantage of a new UCI regulation which would allow a composite team – that is, a group of pros who normally ride for different sponsors – to enter the Nissan Classic, the annual tour of the Irish Republic. He organised the team and paid for it out of his own pocket. Why? Because it would be good for him to have a week's competitive training shortly before the six-day season opened. And it would be good for *The European* to be represented in an international event which got a lot of exposure on the Continent. So why didn't his sponsors pay for it? The answer came from Rushton: once a sponsoring company bought a package, it didn't like to be asked for additional funds, however worthy the motive. Doyle, by way of explanation, simply quoted the old commercial tag, 'You've got to speculate to accumulate.'

Tony with his wife, Anne, before the start of the Kellogg's city centre race in Westminster, 1986

In the 1991 Nissan Classic, Doyle leads the Italian Maurizio Fondriest, and the Australian, Phil Anderson, up St. Patrick's Hill in Cork, said to be the steepest residential street in the world. And to get to know it better, the riders have to climb it four times before they finish

13

Colorado Springs 1986. Only Geoff Cooke (left) responds to the joke from Guido Coster. Mick Bennett, Doyle and Pierrot de Wit smile politely

It's not unknown, of course, for leading sportsmen to look to their own advantage. Winning is a selfish business; it can't be otherwise. And nice guys, as they like to remind you, finish last. But there's another side to Doyle which is revealed in his remarkable capacity for building around him a network of friends and helpers – a kind of extended family – to whom he is invariably loyal and generous in return. 'Tony never forgets people,' says Mick Bennett, who voluntarily managed several of Doyle's cracks at the world title, including his successful bid at Colorado Springs in 1986. 'After Colorado a case of champagne arrived at Christmas, and this lovely album of photographs, just thanking me.'

The godfather of that family is Whiteway, now in his 80s, whose help in giving the 14-year-old the right kind of start in cycle racing Doyle has repaid many times over by his continuing friendship. Whiteway is always a guest at the Doyles' house on Christmas day, and Doyle remains a conscientious chairman of Clarence Wheelers. 'He's got this great concern for elderly people,' says Bennett. 'He's got quite a close attachment to my father, who is 80. Always when he speaks to me he asks, how's your dad? He's very hard in lots of ways, but deep down is this soft, sentimental, almost romantic sort of person.'

In the same year as Colorado, Whiteway had a road accident which put him in hospital. Over the few weeks of his absence, Doyle went to the house where Whiteway lived alone and, with the help of his younger brother, Gerard, and some other club members, cleared it out and decorated it from top to bottom. He had the place rewired, got a phone installed, bought a television set and a fridge, which he stocked up ready for the convalescent's return. Then he went off and won the world title. None of which good works, I might add, has ever been mentioned by Doyle himself.

Second in length of service, I suppose, would be Paul Wingrave, who has been Doyle's regular derny driver since 1980. A derny is a motor-assisted cycle which is used on the track as a pacing machine – a sort of mobile wind-break – in certain specific races, or in training where a rider wants to build up his suppleness by pedalling at speed. It was for this second reason that Doyle called up Wingrave shortly after he had ridden his first Six at Wembley. Knowing he had several more contracts lined up, but that there were gaps between them, Doyle wanted to keep up his form at Herne Hill.

Motor-pace driving, either on the derny or the big motor, is as much a sport to Wingrave as racing is to Doyle. He is Britain's leading specialist, though curiously he doesn't have a motorbike licence and can't drive on the road. And although his father was a cyclist, he raced only two or three times himself as a schoolboy. But he grew up in the sport and has a natural understanding, refined by years of experience, with the riders whose legs are going like a piston in his wake. He is also self-employed – he and his brother have a business, Security Grille Protection – so that although he

15

works long hours he can usually get away for a spell at the Herne Hill or Reading tracks.

At first it was a professional service for Doyle. But the following summer, when he was at Herne Hill helping Doyle tune up to defend his world pursuit title in Brno, Wingrave's engine suddenly cut out. Doyle crashed into the back of him and slid along the track. His legs and buttocks were so badly flayed – the grazes also becoming infected – that he had to cry off from the championships. 'Although it was not my fault, I felt so guilty, and I knew how much it had cost him, that I said I wouldn't take any more money from him until he had won his title back. And that's how it's gone on ever since. Even though he did win again.'

So why does he do it?

Because I like him. Because Tony's that sort of personality, I suppose. He's easy to get on with. He treats you fairly. He doesn't treat you like a mug. I mean, if he rings up and says he wants to train at ten, and you say you can't get away until twelve, he'll say, all right, we'll make it twelve.

And the other thing is, he's a true professional, and that adheres you to him. We sponsored him for a couple of years early on. He always kept us fully informed about what was happening. He got this big picture blown up so that we could hang it in the office and people would know what we were doing. And if he got an interview on the radio or anything, he would always try to mention us. He's a great one for self-publicity, but he does consider his sponsors. A lot of riders, they just ride. They wouldn't dream of doing anything like that.

Then there's the overseas member of the 'family', who has seen Doyle through six-day races and world championships much as Whiteway guided him in his first time trials. This is his Belgian soigneur, Pierrot De Wit. A soigneur is to a masseur what a doctor is to a medical orderly, a carer with better qualifications and more responsibilities. It is a respected profession on the Continent, and especially in Belgium, a country which at a typical Six in 1991–92 provided 7 of the 12 soigneurs at the track. De Wit is the doyen of them all. He is 58, and before he settled for spending the winters at the Sixes and devoting his summers to his private practice in Brussels, he was involved in all the major tours and the Olympics. The list of riders he has looked after is a roll-call of post-war championships: André Darrigade, Jacques Anquetil, Rik Van Looy, Walter Goodefroot, Eddy Merckx; and the legs that he has massaged have pedalled their way to 31 world titles.

De Wit has had Doyle as a client since the Milan 6 in 1984, and when Doyle is racing in Belgium he generally stays at De Wit's house in Brussels. Although in the winter of 1991–92 De Wit was also looking after the Belgian, Stan Tourné, and the German, Roland Gunther, it's clear that he hits it off

16

best with Doyle; they are, he says, more like father and son. It's partly a matter of shared experience: De Wit was at Ghent with Doyle in 1988 when a foul-up in the arrangements cost him a virtually certain world title, and again when he crashed at Munich a year later. Doyle earned his sympathy in one event, his admiration in the other. 'He is a fighter. To be so close to death and still come back. To be two weeks in a coma ... But later when I went to visit him in London I was amazed. I could see it in his eyes that he would come back.' De Wit has a low estimate of most of the riders on the circuit, but Doyle is different. He is generous, and 'he respects the personnel.'

What Doyle in particular respects in De Wit is that he, too, is 'serious' about cycling. Even in his late fifties he still races through the summer, and in 1991 won 19 gentlemen's – or veterans' – events. What he provides at the Six is massage, medical treatment (after consultation with a doctor), advice on diet, preparation and training, tactical prompting during the race and all-round moral support. 'It's fifty per cent work, and fifty per cent psychology. I know when he is nervous and I have to leave him alone.' But more than that, Doyle treats De Wit almost as a manager, meeting him even before the season begins, to discuss his racing programme. It is part of Doyle's gift to involve others, and De Wit's response is typical. He no longer needs to continue in the Sixes; his practice in Brussels is enough. But provided that he can drop out from time to time – with his son, Stefan, standing in for him – he will continue to look after Doyle for as long as he wants to go on racing. Then, when they have both had enough, they will retire simultaneously.

Before that happens Doyle hopes that he will be able to ride a Six before his own public again. And the news that Manchester is to build an indoor cycle track as part of the city's bid for the 2000 Olympic Games brings that possibility closer. It was a blow to Doyle that the Wembley 6 closed immediately after his début there. Since then any fans who wanted to watch him do what he does best have had to travel to the Continent. Many thousands have done so over the years. But that doesn't compensate for his loss of a home fixture – with the publicity, the pull with promoters and the simple gratification that would have brought him. Of course, says Doyle, with the Olympics going open he might compete in them himself. He's joking, naturally. Or then again, perhaps he is not.

17

A winter's tale 1

Before the six-day season of 1991–92 began, I asked Tony Doyle if he would keep a diary of his winter. The point was not to give a blow-by-blow account of each day's racing, but to jot down anything that struck him, trivial or significant, about his life as a rider on the six-day circuit. Conscientious as ever, he invariably kept the diary up to date, often writing his notes on odd scraps of paper in the early hours between leaving the track and dropping off to sleep.

The season should have started on October 16 with the first Six ever to be staged in Moscow. But then came the coup against President Gorbachev and, uncertain which way the political wind was blowing, the organiser, Frank Minder of Bremen, and his German sponsors thought it prudent to postpone the experiment. instead the winter series opened eight days later and more conventionally in the north German city of Dortmund, which was holding the golden jubilee of its Six.

When they signed their contracts, Doyle and the Australian, Danny Clark, understood that they would be partners at Dortmund. This pleased them both since they had won 9 of their last 10 Sixes together. Instead they found themselves paired with two promising but minor German riders in opposition to the two most powerful of them, Andreas Kappes and Olaf Ludwig, who were obviously the promoter's candidates for victory.

DORTMUND 6

Thursday, 24 October

I was keen to get back to the unnatural job I revel in, and particularly eager to return to Dortmund where I have won three times.

In the run-up to the winter programme I felt like a schoolboy returning after the long holidays. School out for summer but no absconding during the winter. It's the same school with the same teacher, same lessons and same old faces among the soigneurs, riders, mechanics and runners. Maybe just the odd newcomer in the class of '91. All in all, it was like never having been away. At once you stepped right back into the underground world of six-day racing.

One big change: the riders have moved up in the world from the old, less lavishly-furnished section of the Park Hotel to the expensive, modernised seventh floor. From the dungeons to a penthouse. How the riders' stature has improved in the space of a year.

We kicked off the first night with a lavish laser show starring members of the cast of Andrew Lloyd Webber's *Starlight Express*, which has recently opened in Dortmund. A real touch of glitz before the introduction of the teams. The show and the improved hotel accommodation must be the promoter's way of celebrating the jubilee.

I had the task of acting as taxi-driver to a young apprentice partner, Thomas Dürst. Since I passed my 'knowledge' years ago, this should have given Dürst a faster insight into the way things work. But after the kick-off it soon became clear that I was going to be in for a long six days. There was the familiar panic brought on by the speed and the danger as teams tried to slot into the fray, and Dürst was finding it tough going. By the end of the night the top candidates to win at Dortmund had already shown themselves. But we weren't among them, in fact we were in last place; I knew that I was going to be watching from the sidelines.

Friday, 25 October

A very enthusiastic crowd watched the second night's racing. It is amazing how immune you become to the intense noise, the thick, polluted air and the stench of frankfurters, burgers and fried onions and Dortmunder Union Bier. Peace, quiet and fresh air do not abound in the six-day world.

My partner, Dürst, has really been in for a shock. Completely shattered halfway through the evening, he was forced into an early retirement. A well-respected, up-and-coming professional with the PDM outfit, he is far from a novice. He was previously with Panasonic, and before turning pro won an amateur Six and rode the track in the Olympics. But the pace and pressure at Dortmund were more than he had bargained for. I had to ride on alone until I was teamed up with Carsten Wolf whose partner, Remig Stumpf, didn't dare to go far from a flush toilet. You have to be able to adapt.

Saturday, 26 October

In the Sixes, Saturday is known as 'the Golden Night'. Traditionally the racing is faster, a full house is guaranteed, and promoters from other events are watching with keen eyes. Riders' wives and girlfriends, families and fans all merge together to make the racing more intense.

This session at Dortmund was typical, 15,000 spectators really making for a great atmosphere. It was good to see some of the former champions turning up – Rik Van Steenbergen, Patrick Sercu, Sigi Renz, and two other popular home riders, Gustav Kilian and Didi Thurau. Kilian, one of the giants of the six-day world, had just celebrated his 84th birthday but looked 25 years younger. He is still active, regularly riding his bike; he had covered 80km that morning. Thurau, always a showman, caught everyone's eye by parking his Ferrari Testarossa in a prime spot so that all the riders going to the track had to walk past it. It was his first visit to a Six since his retirement at Stuttgart in January 1989.

19

Racing went on to 3.13 am, and this being a Saturday night, Danny Clark sang a couple of songs. 'Hound Dog' got the crowd going, and the riders thought it was pretty appropriate.

Sunday, 27 October

Sunday, a 'day of rest' for a lot of tired legs. We were not in bed until 4.30 am and back on the track at 12.30 pm. But at least it was a short session, over by 6.30 in the evening. Many of the riders were suffering from stomach upsets and diarrhoea, and Otto Seiger, the race director, is wondering whether it's due to conditions in the riders' kitchen or to a virus.

Sieger is a real character, a ex-POW and ex-pro six-day rider from Berlin where he runs a chain of petrol stations. He is very enthusiastic and friendly and has mellowed with age.

Everyone was looking forward to a long rest in the evening. It was a chance, too, for some to go home for the night. Etienne De Wilde was returning to Belgium to make a surprise appearance on a TV programme about how the wives of bike riders spend their lives. And I was hoping that Anne had been able to get a seat on a plane to fly out. We were in luck; she turned up later at the hotel.

Monday, 28 October

After a longer night's rest than usual, it was back to a typical day begining at 11.15 am. Breakfast in the riders' kitchen at 11.30. Had a long, relaxing

His partnership with Clark interrupted in 1989, Doyle finds himself acting as taxi-driver at Bremen to the much-admired German veteran, Didi Thurau, with whom he comes fifth

chat with Danny Clark. It was nice not having to rush my food.

After breakfast went to the massage cabin to see Pierrot, and to have my main massage for approximately an hour. Began to psych myself up for tonight's racing when my sponsors were coming along to watch for the first time. After the massage back to my room to read and make phone calls and to sleep. Up again at 4 pm, a cold shower to wake me up. Then at 4.45 pm ate the main meal of the day: salad, pasta, chicken and rice and so on. Came back to my room for a short time, then had to meet journalists and sponsors. Talked until 7.30 pm, had to dash to get ready for the next night shift.

Monday in Germany is traditionally a girls' night out, and known as the 'Hookers and Hairdressers'. The place was filled with young girls out to enjoy themselves. And because of their enthusiasm the racing, and our pain, was extended to 3 am instead of the normal 1–1.30 pm.

The evening was marred by a crash during the first chase when five riders came down. Two of them, Peter Pieters, who was leading the race until then, and Michael Haase, a newcomer to the pros and to the six-day world, needed hospital treatment. For once I was lucky, thank God.

The music is being provided by the Tornados, a band who have been regulars at Dortmund since 1984. You get to know what time it is, and how much racing is left, by the particular tunes they are playing. Particularly on the fifth night and after you have listened to them for eight years. I am a real regular at Dortmund.

Tuesday, 29 October

One Golden Jubilee Dortmund 6 under my belt. A very hot, keen crowd cheered the local boy, Rolf Aldag, to victory with Danny. Peter Post was here to start the final chase, and see Danny equal his record of 65 wins. News arrived here that the Moscow 6 is now a cert for December, so lots of speculation among the riders and personnel about what to expect.

All that spoilt the result was Pieters's crash. After being carried away by stretcher he apparently needed stitches in a cut on his forehead. It just goes to show the need to wear a shell helmet. Peter didn't, unfortunately, and it may have cost him his first six-day victory.

A stunning laser show rounded everything off. As I had time to wind down after the race I went to look at an exhibition on the 50-year history of the Dortmund 6.

Result: 1 Danny Clark (Australia)/Rolf Aldag (Ger), 481pts; 2 Kappes/Ludwig (Ger), 447pts; 3 Gorgen (Ger)/Pieters (Hol), 423pts; 7 Doyle (GB)/Tourné (Bel) at 6 laps

Munich 1990, and the ordeal of Doyle's return is over. He receives a congratulatory kiss from Anne

Chapter 2

Crash!

At 11.15 pm on Sunday 12 November, 1989, Tony Doyle's season – and very nearly his career as a six-day cyclist – came to grief in a crash at the Olympiahalle in Munich. It happened on the fourth night of the Munich 6, and in the second and longer of the two madison sessions when each team was straining to defend its position in the race and, if possible, gain laps on the rest of the field.

Doyle had just gone on the attack and was accelerating anti-clockwise round the banking and into the back straight when, just ahead of him and without any visible warning, the Russian, Marat Ganeev, switched to his right. It was impossible for Doyle to avoid him. Almost stopped dead by the impact, he toppled and slid down the track, falling head-first among the trackside chairs and hitting the concrete floor. He immediately lost consciousness. Five other other riders fell, two of them needing hospital treatment, but Doyle had by far the most serious injuries.

For several days it was uncertain whether he would survive the bruising to his brain and the threat of a haemorrhage. And even when the immediate danger passed, and over the next next weeks and months a dangerous lung infection cleared, the several fractures of his right shoulder and elbow knitted, and his grazed skin healed, it still seemed almost inconceivable that he would ever again cycle with his old confidence and fluency. Or that he would return to ride at Munich the following year. And especially that he would win there.

In fact the collision itself was only the first of not so much a chapter as a bound volume of accidents, which did little credit to the emergency services at the stadium. In the event Doyle's physical recovery from their effects, and his grafting resolve to get back on his bike and race again, were remarkable even in a sport where riders regularly fall and rise like Tumbling Kellys.

Up to the moment of the crash, Doyle's season had gone only moderately well. The promoters, who have always reserved the right to mix and match the riders as they choose, had decided that his fruitful partnership with the veteran Australian, Danny Clark – five wins together the previous winter, three of them on the trot – had become too much of a good thing, discouraging for local riders and therefore bad for business.

So Doyle had found himself starting off the season in Paris with Pascal Lino, a French road rider pretty new to the six-day track. And while Doyle was very pleased with his own form, they had finished no higher than fifth. Dortmund had been more encouraging: he had come second with the German, Torsten Rellensmann, European motor-paced champion for the past two years – a good, accomplished trackie, but still not recognised as one of the top six-day riders. Then at Grenoble it was back to fifth place with another Frenchman, Jean-Claude Colotti, an excellent finishing sprinter on the road but again inexperienced on the track.

Doyle had no reason to feel discouraged. He knew he was going well and, considering the quality of his partners, he had achieved respectable placings. But Munich, his fourth event, promised better things. For the first time that season he would have a top six-day rider, Urs Freuler, as his partner. A laconic but highly competitive Swiss, Freuler had won stages in the Tours of France and Italy, and on the track had virtually monopolised the world points championship, taking the title eight times in nine years. He also had to his credit almost as many six-day wins as Doyle. They had never ridden together before, but were well matched in ability, Freuler's bursts of speed complementing Doyle's sustained efforts as a pursuiter, and also in ambition. Freuler, too, had just two second places and a fourth to show for the season so far, and was equally keen to finish first at Munich, which Doyle describes as the blue riband of the Sixes.

Midway through the fourth evening they seemed to have every chance of doing so. They were lying second to Andreas Kappes and Etienne De Wilde, on the same lap and only three points behind, which was nothing. And they were fighting strongly.

Doyle can recall the events of the evening up to the hour's chase:

I can remember winning the team devil, which was just prior to the chase, and doing the lap of honour. I can remember meeting two British journalists from the *Observer* who had come over, Bob Holmes and the photographer, Mike King. But the accident I can't remember, or the actual madison prior to it. And that's common practice, I've been assured by the doctors. It's your body's way of helping you forget the trauma it's been through. They say I won't ever remember exactly what happened.

Doyle's mental picture of the crash, then, has been formed from other people's accounts of the incident, and from what his own experience tells him it must have been like.

Everyone's told the same story, which has assured me that this is what actually happened. After 43 minutes of the madison I was lying third or fourth in the string of riders. I'd just been thrown into the race by Freuler. And I'd attacked, broken clear of the pack to try and gain a lap, and I was overtaking as I was attacking.

I came up to the rider who was leading, Ganeev, and as I came to draw almost alongside him, he turned up and ran straight into my path. No way I could miss him. I'd have been going like 36mph. And he'd have been doing 33–34mph as he did his right-hand turn straight into me. Normally it's an unwritten rule that as you swing up the track you look over your right shoulder to check that nobody's coming along and the track is clear. He didn't look over his shoulder, didn't indicate.

Here Doyle's natural facetiousness breaks through: 'No hand signal, no blinkers. He just wiped me straight out.' Ganeev, then 24 years old, was an accomplished rider and used to maneouvring on a crowded track; in 1987 he had won the world amateur points title in Vienna. But this was the first winter that Soviet cyclists had been able to compete as professionals, and so Ganeev was new to the conventions of the six-day circuit. He has never denied that, through inexperience, he was at fault in the affair, though he says he tried to indicate with his elbow that he was about to move right. Doyle's belief, backed by the unanimous verdict of those riders and spectators who witnessed the incident, is that no warning was given. Doyle continues his account:

The way I hit him, meant that I came straight down and fell from the track. Normally when you come off you go into a slide, maybe for 10 or 15 metres, 20 metres even. It always looks horrific to the public, but because it's a wooden track, nine times out of ten the crash appears worse than it actually is. On this occasion I was almost stopped cold and when I hit my head on the concrete floor, I was out, I was unconscious.

That's as far as he can piece it together. Some reports say that another rider ran over him after he fell, but Doyle doesn't know whether it's true or not. The Six was being televised by a local cable network every evening, but later when Doyle, in his effort to understand the accident, asked to see their film, they said they had nothing to show him. At first he thought that might be for fear of getting involved in a compensation claim. But he now accepts that, having only a couple of cameras focused on the bends, they simply missed the crash.

There was pandemonium because another six riders came down as well.

I know that I was lying beside the track, and obviously the doctor and the Red Cross came rushing over, and all my helpers – my soigneur, Pierrot De Wit, my mechanic, Bob Arnold, and Bon-Bon, my runner. And when the rest of the riders got off their bikes, Danny was there to see what he could do.

I was put on a stretcher, which took a while, and I was left there, still in all my cycling kit. They didn't cover me up. Finally they began to take me out of the velodrome. But as they tried to carry me down into the exit tunnel below the track, one of the bearers slipped, lost his grip on the stretcher, and dropped me onto the concrete steps. According to one of the German newspapers I fell three metres. And the way they put me back on the stretcher was just as bad. I'd already damaged my right side, and when they went to pick me up they lifted me by my broken right shoulder. It might have been worse if I had been a tennis player or a librarian ... Librarian?

Putting books back on the top shelf ... but the shoulder certainly isn't as mobile, flexible or strong as it used to be.

Sigi Renz, the race director and a leading six-day rider of the 1960s and 1970s, said, 'I've never seen such chaos before.' And the Munich paper, *SZ*, described how the accident, 'the worst in the history of the six-day ... paralysed the spectators'. Watching the unbelievably inept display by the attendants from the Bavarian Red Cross, relayed live on the giant video screen in the hall, there were 12,000 people whistling in protest and derision. But even then they didn't see the final stage in this sorry episode. Doyle again:

I was still uncovered as they went to take me out of the velodrome. I'd been racing that night for nearly four hours in front a big crowd. And obviously you're sweating, it's very hot. Well, they took me to a door where there was supposed to be an ambulance waiting, but in fact the ambulance was waiting at another door. So then they carried me round the outside of the stadium. It's now gone midnight, and it's sub-zero. This is Munich in November. And I'm still uncovered. Once they had got me to the ambulance and I was taken to Bogenhausen hospital, I was superbly looked after. It was just the hoohah of getting me onto the stretcher and into the ambulance that caused a bit of a problem.

Meanwhile at the stadium racing had stopped while the injured were cared for. The German, Markus Hess, who had broken his elbow, and the Dane, Jens Veggerby, suffering from concussion, were taken to hospital, while Ganeev, Roland Günther and Alfred Achermann were treated at the track-side for bruises, burns and abrasions. The chase was not the last scheduled event of the evening; there should have been motor-paced racing and sprints to come. But even those who had avoided the pile-up were shocked and upset, and shortly after midnight the day's programme was abandoned.

All the same the riders closed ranks and resumed next day. Doyle's partner, Freuler, would not reproach Ganeev: 'It's fate. We know that novices represent a high risk to us, but you've got to accept people. I used to make mistakes too.' He was given a new partner, his countryman, Hans-Rudi Marki, with whom he finished fourth. And Kappes, who also refused to apportion blame – 'It could happen to any of us. Yet again it shows how dangerous six-day racing is' – went on to win with De Wilde.

Not that Doyle was aware of any of this. He was lying in a coma in the intensive care unit at Bogenhausen. He was found to have broken the scapula of his right shoulder in five places and the radius of his right elbow in two. He had severe bruising and lacerations and also needed a couple of stitches in his elbow. Serious head injuries included bruising to the brain. He also had a lung infection, which commonly occurs after concussion, and because he couldn't breathe unaided, he was on a ventilator.

With a bad head injury you don't know which way it's going to go. So I had to have constant surveillance, be constantly monitored. Anne and my sister, Janet, who's a nurse, were there all the while. And it was eight days before my condition stabilised and I showed any flicker of regaining consciousness. Even then I didn't come to properly, just opened my eyes for a few seconds. But it proved to them that I was attempting to regain consciousness, and so they allowed me to fly home.

Few people at home had realised what bad shape Doyle was in. News of the crash was too sketchy and arrived too late to be given any prominence in the Monday papers, and completely missed the next edition of *Cycling Weekly*, which is prepared for printing at the weekend. And the only two eye-witnesses from the British press had to wait another week before they could publish their words and pictures in the *Observer*. The Doyle family, always a close unit, discouraged any sort of publicity, not knowing what the outcome of the injuries might be. And in that they were abetted by Alan Rushton, head of the promotional firm, Sport for Television, who had been Doyle's friend and, with varying degrees of formality, his business adviser over the past seven years.

Rushton, for Doyle's sake and his own, also had other reasons for feeling relief that the news hadn't broken more dramatically. He was in the middle of negotiating with Ever Ready-Halfords what he hoped would be a new three-year contract for an eight-man team led by Doyle.

It was only by chance that he learned of the crash sooner than most. Realising that he been out of touch with Doyle for ten days or so, which was unusual, he tried to phone him at his Munich hotel. Instead he was referred to the hospital: 'It was terrible. He had fallen the day before, he was on life support and we didn't know how bad he was.' If Rushton was worried about Doyle's condition, he was also concerned about the Ever Ready-Halfords deal. 'If they heard that he was crocked, well, that was eight jobs per annum, 20 man-year jobs, 30 if you count the support.'

Doyle came back by air ambulance to RAF Northolt, and was rushed straight through to intensive care at Charing Cross Hospital, where he spent the initial week before being transferred to the neuro-surgical ward for the next five weeks. Charing Cross had been recommended by Dr Andy Coady, who worked at the hospital and had been Doyle's friend over many years. He was an ex-bikie himself; when Doyle began racing at the Herne Hill track, Coady, who won national medals in the sprint and the kilometre, was already a member of the British squad. Another family connection was that Coady had trained at University College Hospital while Janet was a ward sister there. But Coady's was not the only reassuringly familiar voice that Doyle would hear whenever he struggled awake. He would be directly under the care of Dr Wolfgang Kox, whom he also knew because of the doctor's interest in sports medicine. It was only seven weeks after the crash that Doyle's memory began to come back bit by bit:

> It wouldn't all come back for a further three weeks, and even then it wouldn't come back clearly. And apart from the effect on my mind, the accident had been a major shock to my whole body. Although I was slowly recovering, I couldn't exercise at all, being bed-ridden for so long. I also had difficulty swallowing because of the after-effects of the ventilator. I couldn't eat and drink properly, and obviously I lost a lot of weight. And damage to my throat meant I couldn't speak for four or five weeks.

It was when Rushton went to see him at Charing Cross that he appreciated the extent of Doyle's injuries:

> And now with all the journalists phoning for information we decided to clam up. On various grounds. He wasn't speaking to us. He was practically unconscious best part of the time. If you say an athlete is like that you're writing him off. And we didn't want to do that because it was his commercial future we were writing off – for the sake of a story, or for being frank. So we said he's in hospital and not talking to anybody. He can't come to the phone, the doctors say he's got to take it easy.
>
> Well, it wasn't like that at all. The guy was sat in hospital practically unable to recognise you when you came in. It was a darkened room with sackfuls of mail in it after people found out where he was. He'd lost I don't know how many stone. He was gaunt, unshaven, yellow, and looked at you in a really difficult way. He was in a very, very bad way, totally

vacant. It was awful. Eventually he was able to shuffle round the ward, and he got his humour back. But until shortly before Christmas he was still uncoordinated and his speech was slurred. And then all of a sudden, over a period of two days, he changed. He moved from being slumped in the bed, totally despondent, to "Hello Alan, nice of you to come." We were all jumping around the place, it was terrific.

Anne, in her calm and dependable way, was also coming to terms with the uncertain nature of Tony's recovery:

Until then I didn't know anything about brain injury. I suppose I thought that once you regained consciousness that was it. I didn't realise that it needed months and months of relearning, that normally the whole process might take a few years. Only afterwards I came to appreciate that the speed at which Anthony got well was so exceptional.

Because Doyle's improvement was apparently slow and erratic – one day's hopes often followed by disappointment on the next – people recall different turning points. Mick Bennett, a close friend who had won a chestful of medals with the British pursuit team in the 1970s, and who had helped to organise many of Doyle's world championship bids, explained:

I always spoke to him as if it was him, if you know what I mean – as if nothing had happened. And there was a time when he couldn't be shaved, just didn't want it. So I said I'll have a bash. I remember sitting him in a chair and lathering him up. It must have been very sore, for suddenly he just knocked the razor out of my hand and said, "oh, fuck it". And that's when I knew that he was going to come out of it.

Anne and the family, however, date the real turning point to New Year's Eve. Doyle had been allowed one weekend visit home before, out of frustration, he had discharged himself from Charing Cross on 23 December. It was a low-key Christmas: visits from the family but dinner alone with Anne when, although she had to cut up his food for him, he had sat at table for the first time. It was a faintly remembered step in the progress which continued, from 27 December, at a rehabilitation centre in Unsted Park, Godalming, 20 miles away. There he was to remain for nearly two months.

He was home again for the New Year weekend, and on 31 December, after an unusually long, deep sleep, his self-awareness seemed to return overnight: 'I woke up, and that was it. I started asking questions and didn't stop. I said to Anne, get me the cuttings, I want to look at them. And then I rang up every member of the family, and asked them all the same questions: what happened? how long was I in intensive care? what was I like?' That evening he insisted on paying a surprise visit to his parents. His mother says that, to her amazed delight,

> He phoned up earlier, and said, "What are you having for dinner?" So I said, "Roast beef and Yorkshire pudding and roast potatoes." So he said, "I'm coming." Then Anne came on the phone and said he wants to, but he won't be able to. He'll have to go to bed. Then a little later there was a knock on the door. And he even stooped down, because he's so tall we'd have seen him through the glass. And Anne said, he was determined to come round.

He paid for the effort with extreme tiredness the next day, but although from then on he had good days and bad, he improved steadily: 'That's when I started to piece things together. It was still a sort of Jekyll and Hyde situation and I never knew who I'd wake up as, but two or three weeks later I could go through a day without spells when I'd fall asleep.'

At Unsted Park he started with the most basic exercises:

> I had to get movement back into my shoulder and into my right side generally. And just get back to a normal routine, looking after myself, washing, and eating with a knife and fork, everyday things. Even learning to write again because I hadn't been able to hold a pen in my hand.
>
> I went through physiotherapy, you know, exercise and games with a football or a tennis ball or a badminton racket. I spent a lot of time doing exercises in the swimming pool. And then I'd be given computer games to get me to use my damaged right side. It was all very gradual. I was fully conscious, but I tired easily and had a very short concentration span. I had no idea of the time, for instance.

His rehabilitation was undoubtedly helped by his attitude of mind:

> I knew I'd had a very serious accident, but right from the outset I also knew I was going to make a full recovery. I don't understand why but I was sure I was going to be OK. I was never bitter or angry. I never asked myself, why did it have to happen? Why me? Even though it was going to cost me so much money in lost six-days, I never felt bitter or frustrated. Mind, I'm sure the fact that the crash was caused by somebody else's mistake helped me come to terms with it. If it had been my fault I would have found it that much harder to accept.

Doyle is a practising Catholic, and friends believe he has taken his religion more seriously since his accident. It's not something he mentions unless he is asked, but he accepts that it helped to shape his approach:

> Yes, I feel that I was very fortunate that my guardian angel was looking out for me that night in Munich. I know that belief played a role in my

recovery, unquestionably. I was relatively young, I was extremely fit, and so doctors gave me a chance of a very good recovery. But nobody thought it would be so complete or would come so quickly. Yes, I have to say that I have been looked after.

For those who saw him only at long intervals, the improvement in his condition must have been remarkable, though for Doyle it was an almost imperceptible progress.

I never put myself under pressure by saying that I had to get back on the bike by the month of May or whenever. I knew that I had to be very patient and never gave myself any deadlines. Everything was going to fall back into normality as long as I took my time. It never crossed my mind that I wouldn't get back to racing.

While I was at the rehabilitation centre I said to all the therapists, just get me back to being fit enough to lead a normal life and take care of everyday things. Don't worry about getting me fit enough to race again. I'll take care of that. I'm a professional cyclist, and it's down to my training on a bike, my hard work, to get me back to racing. I believe they understood. My attitude was that I still had a long career left. So the fitter I was the quicker my injuries would respond and the sooner I'd be able to cope with things on or off the bike.

After starting off with basic physiotherapy and simple exercises in the gym he got on an exercise bike for the first time. At first he could manage only five or six minutes before he was totally exhausted, but gradually increased this to 15 minutes. And towards the end of January he was managing to put in an hour a day in three or four sessions. 'I felt really good about it. And after I'd achieved that, I thought, well you're slowly getting there. But the exercise bike was nothing like a racing bike, so I got on a turbo-trainer several times a day. I built up to an hour-and-a-half or two hours a day while I was still at the centre. Monotonous, but it had to be done.'

It was also at the centre that he first got back on a real bicycle. Not exactly the stripped-down machine he was used to riding,but a mountain bike. The doctors, still worried about the damage he had done not only to the bones but to the nerves of his shoulder, wouldn't let him go out onto the road straight away. A fall on tarmac might have ruined everything. Instead he had to make do with a short ride over the lawns.

But the risks couldn't be indefinitely postponed, so one day before returning home for good at the end of February he pedalled out of the gates of the centre for the first time. He had set himself an hour's run. 'I didn't find the idea at all frightening,' he says,

31

But I had no idea how I was going to feel once I was out, so I got Anne to follow me in the car. Just in case I got tired or I couldn't get back. I mean I'd spent quite a bit of time on the turbo-trainer, but I hadn't been out in the traffic for months. I also wanted to know how far I had gone, so I got Anne to check the tripmeter on the car.

Once I was out on the bike I had no impression of speed. I just gave myself half an hour out, and then turned back. When I got back to the centre I thought to myself, well, realistically you've probably only done 12–13 miles. If you're lucky, 14 miles. I'd been so long not doing anything. So I went to have a look at the tripmeter, and I couldn't believe it. It was 20.4 miles. I thought, blooming hell. It gave my confidence a tremendous boost.

Next day, when he was at home, Mick Bennett came round and they both went off by bike to ride 25–30 miles round the lanes and through Windsor Great Park. And it was Bennett who had to be pushed along towards the finish: 'He hammered me to death.' That weekend, too, Tony and Anne went down to visit her mother at Swanage, and for the first time he went out on the roads unaccompanied. After just four days he was riding solo once more. 'After that I started training seriously. I wasn't putting myself under too much pressure. I thought I'll just see if I can get back to riding the Sixes next winter. I'll set that as my target. The early events I ride at home will just be a gradual build-up.'

It's hard to imagine how anyone could go through Doyle's experience without losing his nerve. For a time, anyway. But he says it didn't happen. 'I may have been a little bit more cautious, but if I had lost my nerve I wouldn't have gone back to racing at all. And I certainly wouldn't have gone back to riding on the indoor tracks.'

The event he chose for his comeback was the first round of the Scottish Provident series of inner-city races. It was at Portsmouth, little over an hour's drive from home, which meant he didn't have to commit himself until the day of the race. In other respects it wasn't the ideal choice. A criterium on a small, tight circuit requires a great deal of concentration, the more so when, as on this particular evening, it is pouring with rain. And the fact that it was the opening shot of a televised competition could only add to the speed of the racing and the pressure to take risks:

I went and had a look at the circuit and thought, well, you're going to have to go back to it some time, so best get it over with. And though, with roads wet and greasy, I was a little bit cautious, I managed to finish the event. And that was a major step.

That was on the Friday, and then two days later, on the Sunday, I rode my first road race. It was the Tour of the Marshes – 125 miles. And

After colliding with Ganeev at Munich in 1989, Doyle lies unconscious on a stretcher beside the track, tended by Pierrot de Wit, and his comrade (though not this time his partner) Danny Clark

there I had the first tumble since my crash. Someone fell off right in front of me, and I came down too. No damage, just got back on. But the thing is, having that fall without any serious consequences meant I had got it out of my system. It wasn't something you could plan to do, but I turned it to my advantage. And I gradually built up from there.

Doyle rode nearly all these training races in Britain – the Halfords contract having gone through, by the way, though reduced to one year for reasons only partly to do with his state of health. But in July he did have one continental reunion with his winter colleagues: the Six-Day of Bassano, not a true Six but a relaxed programme of mixed racing held on the big outdoor track near Venice where the 1985 world championships were staged.

The day before the races started he noticed Urs Freuler, whom he had not seen or heard from since they brutally parted company at the Olympiahalle, standing by the side of the track: 'I went over to him and tapped him on the shoulder, and he said hello, and that was it.' Doyle knew better than to expect Freuler to be effusive, but even he was surprised to find the Swiss quite so lacking in friendly curiosity. Ganeev was also at the track, and seemed surprised to find Doyle there, but although he has since admitted to others that he was at fault in the crash, neither then nor later did he offer Doyle any direct apology.

Doyle finds him 'a bit guarded and wary'. Riding regularly in the same winter peloton, they pass the time of day, he says. There is no animosity, no great warmth either. If they find themselves rolling around side by side, they will talk about how hard a particular race was, or what gears they should be using for the derny race, which is as far as the Russian's sketchy English will stretch. They exchanged New Year greetings on the track at Cologne, and Doyle, like the rest, congratulated Ganeev on his win in the Moscow 6 in 1991. When it was proposed that the two might form a team at Zurich in 1991, Doyle was quick to veto it: 'It would be like putting Neil Kinnock and John Major in the same party.' But that was more a quotable quote for the press than an expression of real feeling: 'I was never bitter or aggressive about it.' So does he like the man? Doyle considers before he answers, 'He seems fairly pleasant.'

It was at the Night of Vienna, a kind of prologue to the winter season held in mid-October, that Doyle resumed his career on the indoor tracks. He was teamed with Gerhard Zadrobilek, an efficient but unmemorable Austrian roadman who was about to take early retirement from pro racing at 29, and in a short programme consisting of a madison, a devil and a points race, they took second place.

Back on form: Doyle is supported by his mechanic, Hector Zelk, at the start of a derny-paced session at the 1991 Munich 6

35

After that introduction there was little fuss made when Doyle rejoined the circuit (Paris having dropped out of the schedule) at Dortmund in October. Riders who hadn't previously met him at Bassano or Vienna, asked after his health and then took his return for granted. Doyle himself was not that sanguine. He still felt he had to prove himself again in the Sixes. But just as he had plunged back into racing on an unsuitably wet night at Portsmouth, so he lost no time at Dortmund by setting out to take the opening madison: 'That win in the first chase meant a lot to me. I felt as if I had never been away.'

As in the previous year he was paired with the Dortmunder, Torsten Rellensmann, and they finished fifth. Then on to Grenoble for a fourth place with Rik Van Slycke. Again a moderate start to the season with modest partners: 'To a certain extent your final placing is going to be governed by that. It's not possible to carry someone night after night, day after day.'

And so to the emotional climax of the season, back to Munich, and with a partner who would be more than self-sufficient, Danny Clark.

I was really warmly received both by the organisers and the crowd, because they realised the seriousness of what had happened to me. The point is, the German press give a lot of coverage to the six-day scene. I'd been a part of it for *x* number of years. I'd won at Munich two winters before. And I'd not only had this terrible accident, but come back from it. The result was I got a fantastic reception.

Doyle responded by riding to the limit of his means – 'I was really psyched up and single-minded, determined to give a good account of myself.' And with Clark driving for a victory too, the pair were hovering in, or only just outside, the lead throughout the race. An aggressive two-lap gain on the fourth, and usually quiet, Sunday night made their intentions clear. But even so, late on the Tuesday night they were still lying second to Adriano Baffi and Pier-Angelo Bincoletto, the Italians having rejoined them on the same lap, with 447pts to their own 303. Everything hung on their gaining a lap in the final madison, and in a grandstand finish they brought it off with little more than 10 minutes to spare. 'Coming back against the odds like that stands out as the most important event in my cycling career. It means more to me than a world title.'

Not that Doyle had long to savour the moment. The race ended at midnight. Then there was a reception to attend and packing to be done because the Bordeaux 6 began the following evening. He was flying out to Brussels at eight in the morning to catch a connecting flight south. Within 19 hours he would be riding on another track in another country and with a new partner, Pascal Lino. And this time he had to accept second place behind De Wilde and yet another local hero from the road-racing peloton,

Greg LeMond's lieutenant, Gilbert Duclos-Lassalle.

One afternoon between sessions at the Munich track, Doyle had gone back with his wife and sister Janet to visit Bogenhausen hospital and the staff who had treated him. In fact, since he had been in a coma for most of his time as a patient there, this was the first time he had seen it. It prompted no memories. And the blank response wasn't only on his side. A couple of the nurses from the Intensive Care department immediately recognised Anne and Janet from the year before, but who was the man with them? Anne explained to the ward sister.

'No it can't be, it can't be Tony,' she said. Tony insisted that it was. 'It's not possible,' she said. And Tony said, no it's me. 'It's fantastic that you've come back,' she said. And Tony explained that while he had called to thank them, and tell them how grateful he was for what they had done, he was also in Munich because of the Six.

'Oh, you've come back to see all your old colleagues. It must be great. They must really appreciate it.'

'No, I've come back because I'm riding in the race. In fact I'm not just riding in the Six, I'm actually leading it at the moment.'

'She simply couldn't believe it,' says Doyle. 'And I think that's when I realised just how fortunate I had been.'

A winter's tale 2

In the one-day break between finishing at Dortmund and starting his next stint at Grenoble, the French winter sports centre encircled by the Alps and the Chartreuse mountains, Doyle flew back to England. So it was on the plane at Heathrow, as he waited to fly south to Lyons, that he picked up the story in his diary.

At Grenoble he was to be teamed with an old friend, the Dubliner Stephen Roche. The last time they had ridden together was in November 1985 at the Paris 6, where they were leading until Roche crashed in the penultimate chase on the final night, badly damaging his left knee. The injury did not prevent Roche achieving a memorable exploit two years later, when he carried off the Tours of Romandie, Italy and France, and the World Road Race Championship, in less than four months. But the long-term effects of the injury disrupted his career for the rest of the decade.

Both highly competitive riders, they now hoped for a happier outcome: Doyle because he always wants to win, and Roche because he had a special need to do so. He was still without a sponsor for the following season, and success would be a timely reminder that he was still a potential winner in the sport.

GRENOBLE 6

Thursday, 31 October

Whenever I have an opportunity to get home, even for one day, I make the effort. Helps to keep me somewhat sane. Hectic day yesterday after constant phone calls and faxes etc, and sorting out the packing. Managed to get out for 30 miles on the road, the fresh air and the peace and quiet making a pleasant contrast to the indoor track. Looking forward to the Grenoble 6 and teaming up with Stephen. I hope that he is fit and well.

Grenoble last year was really jazzed up and appealed to both the riders and the public, lots of glitz and show. I am well into the groove on my winter treadmill and, feeling confident and relaxed, I don't anticipate any problems. It will be interesting to see how Claudio Chiappucci fares on the boards. I am sure he will make his presence felt one way or another. I just hope that someone is waiting at Lyons to pick me up. Still, I am sure that Bernard Thévenet, the race director, has arranged everything. Last year we felt pampered: 5 star hotel and chauffeurs at our beck and call.

PS at 1.30 pm the following day: Just woke up after the first night's racing at Grenoble. Needed a long sleep after travelling and all the chasing around. Sharing a room with Stan Tourné, one of the 6th form lads. We used up a lot of nervous energy last night during the racing; a good many cowboys and roadmen not accustomed to the boards. I can see there being a few crashes and several lost at sea. I feel that Chiappucci is about as comfortable on the boards as I would be on l'Alpe d'Huez!

Stephen was very, very nervous. Six years is a long time away. But he has so much class I am sure that he will stay.

Friday, 1 November

Well, I finally made the centre stage. I still find it hard to believe that during the middle of a Six, the riders – Laurent Fignon, Stephen and all – should be dancing on the stage with singer Herbert Leonard and his female backing group. The world champion, Michael Hübner, is much in demand. One hundred per cent muscle: the Fred Astaire of the sprinters! I can't imagine this happening anywhere else, but it was effective, and both the riders and the public enjoyed the entertainment.

It is always dangerous with a lot of inexperienced road riders on the track all at the same time. Here you have to pay particular attention, so I wear glasses and contact lenses. Better safe than sorry. It makes you wonder why riders of the calibre of Thierry Marie and Chiappucci are prepared to risk themselves on a 200m track where they are not relaxed or confident.

Each night we also walk round the track to meet various sponsors. But the new modern format is a complete success, with a huge increase in attendance. I wonder what awaits us tonight. Perhaps we'll be asked to go into a cage with the lion tamer.

Saturday, 2 November

A full house. 12,000 people obviously appreciate the new modern format of the Grenoble 6, and local hero, Jeannie Longo, was in fine form, breaking the women's world 5km record just before the pros came on [*that record of 6 min 17.608 sec was ratified the following January*]. It was good, too, to see a special race for the former stars, including Bernard Thévenet, Bernard Vallet, Jean-Pierre Danguillaume, and the clown and darling of the public, Willy Debosscher, as popular as he used to be. The race was a devil, with Willy in his element. The programme was then interrupted for a Sixties-style rock band, and all the riders watched and cheered and danced on the finishing line of the track.

The main chase of the night was a handicap – which also became a handicap for the officials. They found it hard to work out the laps and the team positions afterwards. The riders knew where they were, but the officials had to have the rules and regulations gently explained to them before they understood.

Sunday, 3 November

Well, I am feeling pleased with myself now that I am leading the Grenoble 6 with Stephen. I hope it is not an omen, remembering our last Six in Paris, when after his crash we finished second.

There was a party in the Möet Club (for riders and sponsors) in honour of Vincent Laveneau, who is retiring after the Six. The champagne flowed freely and everyone was able to relax; another rarity in the middle of a Six. I am sure a lot of riders will pay for it tomorrow. Both Stephen and I were on our best behaviour, not just because we were leading the race but because Stephen's wife, Lydia, made sure we went to bed in good time.

Monday, 4 November

Retained the yellow jersey, much to our delight, so let's hope things go with a bang tomorrow. Stephen is very nervous going into the final night, thinking back to the Paris 6. Bruno Saby, the rally driver, appeared at the start with Stephen driving the car. Not how you normally warm up!

Jeannie Longo broke another indoor record, 3-41.291 for the 3km, to add to her tally. What a bike-rider!

A lot of the road riders are looking forward to the close of the Six, because for them it will also mark the end of another season. But we have got another three months ahead of us. I was pleased with how I was going, really flying, no problem except the beginning of saddle sores, which are very uncomfortable. I asked for the doctor here and he told me to wear padded cycling shorts, use a cream and take some Valium – and he's the official medical adviser. A great help, tranquillisers, during the chase.

Tuesday, 5 November

The one that got away. We won the Six but the commissaires thought, why not let the local French boys have the race instead? Where do I start?

At the beginning of the final evening, I suppose, when we set off with the lead, then lost it in the first 20-minute chase to Fignon/Biondi as they came into the same lap with more points. In the final chase, which lasted an hour, there were four teams in contention. But Stephen and I were very determined and rode strongly, and after getting an early lap advantage to regain the lead, we controlled the racing.

With 12 minutes to go Tarentini and Colotti attacked and gained half a lap, but then got stuck there, unable to complete the move. The tempo lifted with the bell lap in sight, and they simply couldn't catch the peloton. The only riders they overtook were two stragglers who had dropped from the field and were 30m behind. And that's how the two Frenchman finished,

They wuz robbed! Stephen Roche and Doyle, wearing the leaders' jersey at Grenoble in 1991 came even closer to winning the Six than they did in Paris

still 20m off the back. Stephen and I were announced as winners, and the other riders came up to congratulate us.

Then the race jury went into a huddle, and after 15 minutes had passed they reversed the decision. We were both stunned, and none of the other riders could believe it either. How could the jury have taken so long to decide whether or not we were caught? There's no argument about it. Either the two Frenchman had caught the group or they hadn't. And they had not. That was clear from the television pictures. The whole thing leaves a bitter taste in my mouth, especially going into the Munich race, the big event of the season.

Result: 1 Jean-Claude Colotti/Philippe Tarantini (Fr), 148pts; 2 Doyle (GB)/Roche (Ire), 146pts; 3 Fignon/Biondi (Fr), at 1 lap

In the short interval before the Munich 6, there was just time to fit in the Geneva one-day omnium where, ironically, Doyle found himself paired with one of the men to whom he had grudgingly yielded first place at Grenoble, Philippe Tarantini. And since one of the events they won together was the madison, Doyle said he found himself shaking hands with him more often and more warmly than he had ever expected.

Chapter 3

Cruel and unusual punishment

Six-day cycle racing was made in England in 1875. Not that anybody recognised at the time that a new sport had been created – no more than William Webb Ellis realised, when he picked up the ball and ran with it 42 years before, that he'd invented rugby football. The six-day race began as a stunt, responding to a popular taste in mid-Victorian England for unusual, sometimes callous, displays of physical strength and stamina. And it took the particular form it did as a compromise with another strong opposing force, which was public respect for the sabbath. Six-day cycling may have evolved since then, but it bears the the mark of its origins to this day.

At this time cricket and golf were well established, but the various types of football had only recently agreed on their sets of rules, and like most of the emerging games – bowls, croquet, hockey, tennis – were still played more for private pleasure than public entertainment. So for the great mass of people sport meant contests of speed and brute force at the racecourse or the racing track or in the ring, with the audience showing little squeamish concern for the well-being of the contestants.

Prize fighting was illegal but still continued in dark corners. In 1860 a bare-knuckle fight between an Englishman, Tom Sayers, and an American, John C. Heenan, was staged on the quiet at Farnborough, Hampshire, and continued into the 42nd round before the mob broke it up. It was the boxers' qualities of strength and endurance that so appealed to 'sportsmen' – a term which cut across all the class divisions – rather than their skill. Professional foot races – in which the runners came to be known as 'pedestrians' – drew far bigger crowds than the football matches which would eventually outstrip them in popularity, and not simply with sprints and middle-distance running. There were novelty races in which the competitors might have to run a mile, walk a mile and then gallop on horseback for a mile. Runners were pitted against dogs, and greyhounds against terriers. Endurance events went to absurd lengths. At Dundee, in a 60-hour running race, the winner was reported to have covered 352 miles.

There was so much of the freak show and the fairground about popular sport that, not surprisingly, cycling followed the fashion. The French-designed 'boneshaker', used in the pioneering cycle races of the 1860s, and the high-wheeled 'ordinary' which succeeded it during the next decade, were – except for horses on certain courses – the fastest means of solo locomotion available. Indeed, in Edinburgh, which had already assumed pride of place in foot racing with its New Year professional meetings at Powderhall, track races between bicycles and trotting ponies became a regular attraction.

So much for stunts, but why the sabbath? Keeping Sunday as a day of rest and religious observance was a custom supported by law. In fact there was a lively debate going on at the time in the cycling journals over whether it was seemly to ride a bicycle at all on Sunday even for recreation or transport. In a letter to *Athletic World* in April 1878, a reader argued that if it was wrong to go for a ride on a Sunday it was equally wrong to go for a walk. He added that a countryman friend of his knew a parson who made any necessary Sunday calls by bicycle, which, to him, seemed to settle the matter. But clearly opposition was strong, and in the case of commercial exploitation, insurmountable.

So if the endurance of cycles and cyclists was to be tested to destruction in front of a paying audience, the longest continuous span in which it could be done was over the six days between midnight on a Sunday night and midnight on the following Saturday. So the six-day race was conceived, and so it has remained, even though the original constraints no longer apply. In fact it's rare for a modern six-day race *not* to run through Sunday, since it's the bigger weekend audiences which put the show into profit.

What is believed to be the first six-day cycling event – you could hardly call it a race – took place in Birmingham in 1875. It was put on by a local manufacturer of ordinaries (better known to us as penny-farthings, though that name only came in when they were on their way out), who wished to demonstrate the reliability of his products. They were ridden for 12 hours a day round a timber-decked oval track, though what distance they covered is not known. A similar event, but with an 18-hour day, was staged in London later in the year. In this case we know the names of the winner, 18-year-old George Waller, and of the runner-up, Charles Terront, a Frenchman who would go on to many victories in Britain and the United States over the next 18 years.

These were essentially sales promotion efforts, and three years passed before the first recognised six-day races were held at the Royal Agricultural Hall in Islington, London, in 1878. It has been suggested that the very first of these was put on there between 29 April and 4 May, and that it was for individual competitors, who rode all the hours they could stay awake. The winner, a man called Smythe, was said to have covered 1,118 miles.

I could find no contemporary record to support this, though a six-day race between runners and walkers was held there at the end of March, and on 13–18 May there was a six-day cycle race of sorts. It was another of those man *v* horse – or as *Athletic World* grandly put it, Bicycling *v* Horsemanship – events. The Agricultural Hall, apart from being used for its stated purpose – the countryside then being just up the road from Islington – was also regularly hired for circuses, athletics meetings, equestrian events and all manner of indoor sports. It was therefore an appropriate place to decide a challenge match between a horseman known simply as Leon the Mexican, who appears to have been an itinerant stunt jockey, and some of the leading professional cyclists of the day.

The promoter put up £200 and a silver cup worth £70 – with supporting prizes down to £15 and a silver medal for fourth – for a Monday–Saturday race of 15 hours a day from 8 am to 11 pm. The racing itself was to be continuous, though the riders could dismount at any time for rest or refreshment and, since the ground was too hard to take tent pegs, wooden huts were built inside the track for that purpose. Or rather the tracks, for two concentric circuits were laid out. The inner one of eight laps to the mile (220 yards/201m) was for the eight cyclists, and seems to have been a pretty makeshift affair; it was knocked together from boards, and when one of the cyclists, Markham, crashed in the sixth lap of his 46th mile, he gashed his arm from wrist to elbow on a projecting nail and had to retire. The outer track, seven-and-a-half laps to the mile, was for the two horsemen, Leon the Mexican having now been joined in the challenge by a man called Newsome of Beverley in Yorkshire.

Newsome seemed a reluctant starter, probably a pressed man, for he was often absent from the race and gradually dropped out of the running. But the heaviest betting was always on the Mexican, who was allowed a relay of 18 horses and on one day changed his mount no fewer than 22 times. He was a relaxed, stylish horseman who paced himself well. Although the leader on the first day was a cyclist, William Cann of Sheffield, and on the second, Phillips of Wolverhampton, Leon was shadowing them closely. On the third day he began to move steadily ahead to run out a comfortable winner by 59 miles and two laps, covering just over 669 miles. Second was Cann with 610 miles, and third Frank White of Wolverhampton, who distinguished himself on one day by riding 150 miles without dismounting – 'a performance without parallel', as the *Bicycling Times* called it – for which the promoter rewarded him with a 'massive gold ring', suitably engraved.

Nowhere was this event claimed to be a first, perhaps because it was seen as no more than a longer version of many similar contests. But neither was there any reference to the Smythe race, which had supposedly been run

45

so recently that some sort of comparison would have been hard to avoid. *Sporting Life* also said in passing that the cyclists racing against Leon had found the going so hard because they had never ridden on so small a track. Would none of them have competed alongside Smythe? The explanation may be that Smythe's event was not a cycle race at all but one of the six-day foot races, or 'wobbles' as they were known. In which case, the first true and undiluted six-day cycle race was probably the one staged – same year (1878), same venue – from 18 November.

This race was put on in conjunction with what was advertised in *Athletic World* as a Monster Exhibition of Bicycles, Tricycles and Bicycling Appliances, offering gold, silver and bronze medals for the best roadster and racing machines on show. The race was for the Championship of the World (well, anyone could say that in those days) and offered £150 in prize money which would soon be 'deposited in the hands of *Sporting Life*'. It would be run under Wolverhampton Rules, which were apparently too well known to need explanation, with riders free to use any size of machine and to change it at will, each being allowed an attendant to help him dismount. Racing would be restricted to 18 hours a day, between 6 am and midnight.

As far as the judging was concerned, the show itself was a disaster. 'The gentlemen appointed to officiate', said *Athletic World*, 'were absolutely incompetent to perform their duties.' And after holding an 'indignation meeting', many of the exhibitors withdrew their products. But the race itself, separately organised by Etherington & Co, bicycle and general advertisers, was a great success. According to the *Bicycling Times*, it attracted far bigger gates than the match against Leon, although 'except when the men spurted against one another, the latter days of the racing were not exciting.' There was also disappointment when Frank White, who had hoped to go for 200 miles without dismounting, crashed and withdrew from the race. But there was no doubt that in William Cann, the runner-up against Leon, the event had a worthy winner. He covered 1,060 and a half miles, only just failing by 7 miles to reach 800 miles in the first four days. 'It was the greatest distance ever done by man's muscular exertion alone in a similar time,' said the magazine's reporter, providing another reason to doubt the authenticity of Smythe's 1,118 miles.

He also offered a few useful programme notes. Cann, he said, was 25, stood 5ft 8 1/2in, weighed 10 stone before starting, and lost 7lb during the race. He rode an ordinary 52-inch roadster, with ball bearings in the front wheel, built by Hydes & Wigfall, the Sheffield firm for which he worked as a bicycle maker. He did no special training beforehand, and only once in his career had he taken time off work to prepare for a race. The runner up, G E Edlin, the 18-year-old son of a Leicester cycle manufacturer, had ridden one of his father's machines, of the same size but with ball bearings front and rear. Although in three years the Six had developed from an exhibition into a genuine contest, it was still being used to advertise company products, and that remains one of the strongest themes of professional racing to this day.

There was another Six in Birmingham that year. It was won by George Waller, who in 1879 went on to make a clean sweep of two Sixes in London and one in Hull, where a six-day walking competition had already been staged. In 1880 London and Hull were joined by Edinburgh, where over the week an estimated 100,000 people were drawn to the track in Waverley Market. All three races went to Terront, who had recently come back from Chicago and Boston after winning two of the first three Sixes to be staged in the United States – the same William Cann having taken the other.

After that, although the six-day craze spread to Australia, and following a short lull picked up again in America, activity in Britain fell away. Newcastle put on three events in the 1880s, and Wolverhampton appeared in the records for the first and last time in 1890, despite the prominence of its riders in other Sixes. In that year, too, Terront won the last Six to be staged in London – or Britain – until the 1920s.

Or, to be precise, the last for men. Towards the end of the century professional women's cycle racing was introduced in London, with regular matches between an English team and one brought over from France. They raced in the intervals between the men's pro events at Olympia, and on a track which had been specially built for them at the Aquarium in Westminster. Serious cyclists – and cyclists could be very serious – wrote dismissively of 'troupes of girls', and there was a conscious touch of vaudeville about the close-fitting catsuits they wore when they raced indoors and the slightly adolescent reception they received from the male audience.

Earning between £25 and £75 a week according to their popularity at the box office, and glamorised by the press, the female teams were often blamed for bringing women's cycling into disrepute. But in their defence the captain of Newhaven Cycling Club wrote, with heavy gallantry: 'Let no one imagine these fair exponents of the whirling wheel as tyros; they are equipped and garbed to meet the challenge of the racing path; their grace and dexterity on the English Velodromes is a tribute to their sex.'

One particular challenge they met was the first and last British women's six-day race, held at Olympia in 1895. It was billed as the Ladies' International Cycling Championship and run as an endurance contest, with four hours' racing daily on a wood-surfaced track of just under 200 yards (201m). The title went to 18-year-old Monica Harwood, already English Lady Champion, who put in 429 miles to beat Mlle Lisette (typically no surname given), the strongest of the French long-distance riders.

So, as with so many of their later inventions, the British lost interest in six-day racing, and the United States took up its commercial development. The men credited with introducing it there, in 1879, were Jack Haverley

The madison relay is still the heart of the Six, and Doyle waits for his partner, Udo Hempel, to throw him into the action on his debut in the Skol 6 at Wembley in 1980

Something more substantial than bread and circuses. Chefs prepare meals for the VIPs in the track centre of a modern Six at the Olympiahalle in Munich

and Peter Duryea, described as two British artists, though probably that should be 'artistes' in the theatrical sense, since what they put on was less a contest than an extended music-hall turn. For six days and six nights they rode in shifts around roller-skating rinks in New York, Chicago and Boston, so that people could marvel at their stamina and the distance they covered. You could even say that they were the first men to ride as a team, but since this wasn't a contest, and they were the only team on the track, their example had been forgotten by the time the idea of racing in pairs was introduced at the end of the century.

What established the Six in the United States was its adoption in 1891 by Madison Square Garden, New York, where, starting as a penny-farthing race but graduating to safety models, it took its place as an annual event among such attractions as Barnum & Bailey's 'Greatest Show on Earth', beauty contests and aquatic exhibitions. The earlier Sixes covered 12 or 18 hours a day, but the version staged in December 1896 was the first with 'unlimited time', starting at a minute after midnight on the Monday morning, following a concert of sacred music which had left the crowd a little restless, and ending at ten o'clock on the Saturday night.

Within that period the competitors could ride or rest as they chose, though the urge to stay in contention for their share of the 10,000 gold dollar prize drove many to the limit of their resources and beyond. In fact not one of the 15 survivors, out of 27 starters, was still on the track at the official finish of the race. The winner, an Irishman called Teddy Hale who was dressed entirely in green, had covered 1,910 miles, and gone home with his lion's share of dollars in his hat, and the rest had been only too happy to follow his example and settle for what they had already won.

One of the stars of the race was 'Major' Taylor, a celebrated amateur sprinter now taking on his first professional engagement. He was only 18 years old and black, and prejudice said that he would never last the pace. But he was a pleasant, well-mannered chap with strong religious convictions (probably the only rider on the track who would have refused to enter if the racing had run into Sunday). He had already scored a popular victory in a half-mile handicap held during the curtain-raising programme on the previous Saturday evening, and once the Six got under way his speed as a sprinter won the crowd over. The regime he had set himself was eight hours' racing to one hour's sleep in his trackside tent – which in comparison with many riders' schedules was self-indulgent. Even so, there were occasions when his trainer had to force him back on the track. None of the riders stopped just to eat. They took their food in pots from their trainers as they rode by, and then threw back their pots when they had finished.

Exhausted riders became more fractious as the event wore on and many began to suffer from delusions. By the last couple of days they were in a shocking state; gaunt, staring and pedalling slowly round the track like automatons. Yet though the racing had deteriorated to a point where it was no longer a contest but a fight for personal survival, the spectators turned up in even greater numbers. The final evening drew a crowd of over 12,000, and the evident public enjoyment of this degrading spectacle, as much as the event itself, brought calls in the press to have it banned.

Even the French cycling paper, *Le Vélo*, which was not above promoting an extremely punishing marathon of its own, the 600km Bordeaux–Paris race, complained of its 'lamentable scenes of horror'. And when there was talk of reintroducing Sixes to Islington, a British cycling journal wrote: 'It is stated that one of the organisers of the Six Days' Torture Races which have been held in New York, is contemplating promoting a similar contest at the Agricultural Hall, London. If he does, we shall use the most strenuous efforts to discourage it in every possible way, and we sincerely hope the British public will show its good sense and good taste by staying away.'

In fact the promoters had trouble enough at home. In 1898 the event was banned, at any rate in its previous form, when the New York State legislature forbade any cyclist to race for more than 12 hours a day. The Garden got round that by introducing teams of two men, so that racing would still be continuous with one or other member of the team always on the track. It was not to be 12 hours on and 12 off; the maximum spell of rest allowed was three hours. And despite gloomy predictions, this arrangement found favour with the public. If there was any nostalgia for the squalor of yesterday, it was lost in new admiration for the feat of the winning team. In six full days Charly Miller and his partner, Frank Waller, covered 4,398km (2,731 miles), which is more than the Tour de France nowadays gets under its belt in just over three weeks.

All the same it's hard to know what to make of the story that the year before, Miller, riding alone, was credited with a distance of 3,797 miles. He was said to have managed on seven hours' sleep during the whole event, but on the fifth day to have stopped long enough to get married in the middle of the arena.

What the new regulations didn't allow for was both riders in a team being on the track at the same time. But that could always be arranged by a little tampering with the concept of 144-hour racing. If the racing was halted for a few hours when even the most avid spectators were on their way to breakfast, then later on, when the crowds came back, the two riders could race together for as long as they had both been resting. And in cities with laxer public regulations, or none, doubling up could be even more easily arranged. So the two-man chase developed: a perpetual relay in which one rider raced around the inside of the track and then, after so many laps, slung his sleeping partner, who had been slowly circling the banking, into the action. And in honour of its birthplace this, the most characteristic and thrilling phase of the Six, is still generally referred to as 'the madison' or racing *à l'Américaine.*

The scene of Doyle's bleakest and best moments in six-day racing

Busman's holiday: on Boxing Day 1991, Doyle lines up in an omnium at Dortmund alongside (l–r) the Soviet rider, Constantine Krabzov, Dutchman Pete Pieters and Gianni Bugno, the Italian world professional road champion who is riding the indoor track for the first time.

Doyle takes a flyer to gain a lap in the 1988 Cologne 6. It is to bring him his fifth victory with Danny Clark that winter

With his soigneur adviser and close friend, Pierrot de Wit, in the massage cabin at Munich 1990, he prepares for the final chase of a Six which will take him back to the top

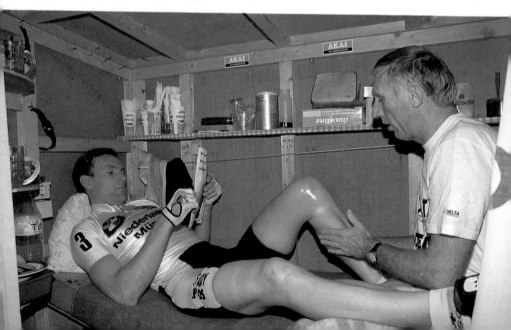

It was as a team event that the Six was reintroduced to Europe – in Berlin 1909, Frankfurt 1911, Brussels 1912 and Paris 1913 – as well as to Australia in 1912, and between the wars became a regular winter attraction in cities right across the United States. Two American stars, Floyd Mac-Farland and Jim Moran, won the inaugural Berlin Six, but once the sport had become established in Europe, there were more French, Belgian, Italian and, particularly, German riders sailing west to compete in the USA than there were Americans making the reverse trip.

In common with the rest of the country, American six-day racing became increasingly isolationist. This did not help its further growth, nor did the fact that promoters were taking too much money out of the sport and putting too little into developing new riders. Even the men who had reached the top felt they were being used. Their racing conditions were more humane than they had been, but were still extremely arduous, and it was as if they were taking part in some freak show like marathon dancing or pole-squatting or roller derby racing. They built up restrictive practices to protect their position, the strongest teams forming combines so that they could share the prizes without having to compete against each other. Eventually this transparent collusion had a disastrous effect on the box office, and outside New York, where Sixes continued off and on until 1961, few of the old regular venues survived the Second World War.

In Europe, where road races and track meetings kept up interest in cycling throughout the year, the Sixes were much more solidly based. With their heavy background music, cabaret acts and non-stop bars, they became the working man's nightclub which fashionable people also patronised, dropping in after an evening on the town for a little earthy entertainment.

Novelist Ernest Hemingway, who lived in Paris during the early 1920s, was fascinated by the track racing he used to watch at the Vélodrome d'Hiver, which he described in his set of autobiographical essays, *A Moveable Feast*. 'I must write of the strange world of the six-day races,' he added. Unfortunately he never did, but in 1923 a French writer, Paul Morand, did record his impression of a Paris Six in these terse notes:

The scoreboard started to work overtime, with some numbers climbing up and others going down. The riders' quarters were concentrated at one end of the track. Each man had a little wooden cubicle with a camp bed sealed off by curtains. A floodlight shone into the furthest corners of the cubicles so that the crowd would not miss a single movement made by their heroes, even when they were resting. The attendants were constantly coming and going in their white hospital coats, surrounded by patches of petrol and grease, mixing embrocations from eggs and camphor... Those who had just been relieved by their team-mates would clamber off their machines to snatch a couple of hours' sleep.

It was very late. The night sprints were over. The contestants pedalled on, palms upward to rest their wrists, and enveloped in balaclavas.

The attempt in 1923 to bring six-day racing back to London was stalled by the discovery that the track put up at Olympia was unsafe. After a week's postponement for repairs the show went on, bringing victory in a close final to the Belgians, Alois Oersyn and Pierre Vandevelde, and sixth place to the only English finisher, Maurice Selbach, who was better known to the cycling public for another and lonelier type of night riding as a triple winner of the North Road 24-hour time trial. The promoters thanked spectators for their support and promised to return the following winter; but they had to wait 11 years for a repeat.

The 1934 Six, again at Olympia, was promoted by the American, Willie Spencer, an ex-rider who travelled across the United States with his portable track putting on cycle races. Knowing that the best way of making a success of his event was to engineer a home win, Spencer was smart enough to pair Britain's best sprinter, Sid Cozens of Manchester, with Piet Van Kempen, the 'Flying Dutchman' (a title inherited by Peter Post), who was already winner of 25 Sixes. The partnership worked and Van Kempen nursed the willing and able Cozens through to victory at the first attempt. Despite the favourable publicity, again no repeat. Two years passed before the next London Six, this time at the Empire Pool, Wembley, which at last led to a run of four brought to an end by the war. No further joy for Cozens, however; with less powerful partners he came away with a sixth and a seventh place, and like other British riders involved – the respected Frank Southall and Charlie Holland, for instance – he was hampered by crashes.

Two more Sixes were put on at Wembley in 1951–2, and then came another long interval before the British Cycle and Motor Cycle Industries Association promoted the first Skol 6 at Earls Court in 1967, with the Dutchman, Charles Ruys, as race director. So began an almost unbroken series of 12 events under the same title, moving on to the Wembley Pool in the following year and dropping out only in 1976 while the Pool was being transformed into the Wembley Arena. There the shrewd Australian bikie-turned-businessman, Ron Webb, was to take over as promoter, and Peter Post, having won four successive Skols with Patrick Sercu, and also begun a new career in management and promotion, was to become race director.

The Skol 6 would have an impact far beyond the northern suburbs of London. It would help launch a number of British cyclists into continental six-day racing – the four-times world pro pursuit champion, Hugh Porter; Tony Gowland, winner of the 1972 Skol with Sercu; the sprinter, Maurice Burton; and, in the nick of time before it dismantled its track for the last time in 1970, Tony Doyle.

Webb recognised that in putting on a six-day race in London he faced a different type of challenge. 'Take the Bremen Six, which is used as the local carnival,' he said back in 1974. 'It draws 90,000 people, but it's doubtful if 30,000 watch the racing. The rest are in the beer halls and barbecue halls and wine cellars.' Keeping people's noses in the trough for long hours was not Webb's concern. For one thing he didn't share in the catering profits. For another, it was not what the public wanted. They were, by and large, members of cycling clubs, and what they demanded was to see their heroes.

Webb's idea, therefore, was to produce a week of varied, non-stop, concentrated racing, revolving round a track only 160m long and enwrapped at either end by 51 degree banking. There was no point in prolonging the agony. The audience was, on average, far younger than it would be on the Continent, and nobody wanted to hang around in Wembley until the dawn broke. And so the Skol programme was based on four evenings' entertainment from 7 pm until the lap of honour was taken just after midnight; a Saturday matinée, plus an evening session which went on until the giddy hour of 1 am; and six hours of racing from 4 pm to 10 pm on Sunday.

The aim was also to make the racing more credible to spectators who wanted to be thrilled by a tight finish but who knew enough about the game to recognise when a sprinter was holding back. One of Webb's problems when he began was the superb showmanship of Post. 'He was so good that his sense of timing was becoming theatrical. Instead of winning a motor-paced race by 10 laps, he would come from behind in the final lap to take it on the line.' Post didn't win by collusion. He could have ridden any challenger off the track. But his attempt to make victory look difficult was unconvincing, and cast an artificial light over the whole proceedings.

Recognising the danger of this, Webb did his best to produce open racing, and there was a particularly thrilling contest between Sercu, the swiftest, silkiest of riders, and a tough, ambitious middle-order Australian, Graeme Gilmore, who took the sprinters' prize two years running. This is not to say that nothing was stage-managed by the riders at Wembley, but the crowd on the whole went away believing what they had seen.

When Webb took his formula to the International Velodrome Union (UIV), the diehards among the continental promoters insisted that he couldn't call the Skol a six-day race although the shortened form, Skol 6, was acceptable. Post introduced the Skol idea at Rotterdam, and was rewarded with a record gate. Frankfurt, Berlin, Dortmund, Munich and Milan followed suit. Within two years the UIV had invited Webb to revise the six-day regulations. Late-night racing with a couple of afternoon performances has now become the norm. And despite certain pockets of conservative resistance like Zurich and Bremen, where sleeplessness is still regarded as a virtue, riders will usually be dead to the world several hours before dawn.

A winter's tale 3

Immediately after Doyle's disappointment at Grenoble came news of the death of Robert Maxwell, owner of *The European*, which had sponsored him since early summer. He was assured that his contract was secure, but he was not in the most serene state of mind as, at the end of another brief visit home, he flew on to Munich. He had already been told that despite an earlier promise, he would not be riding with Clark.

The Munich 6 is held in the Olympiahalle, which housed various indoor events at the 1972 Olympic Games and is now mainly used for trade fairs and exhibitions. For the Six a demountable track is built on a timber frame, with the seating erected around it – the scene of Doyle's frightful crash in 1989 and triumphant return a year later. That was in partnership with Clark, and in that respect there was good news waiting for him in Munich.

MUNICH 6

Thursday, 7 November

On the opening night I was surprised to find that I was paired with Danny, after all, instead of Rolf Aldag, my official team-mate. Just before the start Danny's partner, Olaf Ludwig, had pulled out sick with what turned out to be kidney stones, and so the teams were switched around.

I always look forward to Munich – the race, the atmosphere, the packed house, the track. And, of course, the stadium is full of memories for me, some bad, but mostly good. Now it was my first race with Danny since Munich last year. So I hoped it was a good omen.

It had all been happening to me both at home and at Grenoble. That was a Guy Fawkes night to remember!

Friday, 8 November

Flying ... taking the lead in the Six, winning the big chase and the derny race. I was really motivated and obviously the fact that Anne was coming over helped inspire me. It was also good to see my friends, Dr Andy Coady and his wife, who had come for the Beer Festival as well as the Six. I was surprised to find fans walking around the Halle in *The European* jerseys, which are being sold on one of the bike stands.

Before racing began I wandered around the Halle looking at all the restaurants, discos, bierkellers, car stands, bike displays and the fun fair. It really is six days of complete entertainment. Something for everyone.

Saturday, 9 November

The noise and the buzz – Saturday night, the 'Golden Night', at Munich is unique. Here it is something special, and the adrenalin flows among the riders. A packed house of 15–16,000. Coaches and coaches from Austria, Switzerland and Belgium, and it was good to see that my sister Janet had also flown over for the Six. A complete sell-out with people desperate to get in and prepared to pay three or four times the price of the ticket.

A hard day's racing, with a three-hour afternoon session and then another in the evening from 8 pm to 3 am, so not much chance of a rest. A very knowledgeable crowd, and it's nice to be so popular among the fans.

Sunday, 10 November

Chaos reigned this evening when, during the big chase, the BMW Jagd, smoke started to fill the stadium. At first I thought it was coming either from a barbecue or indoor fireworks. Then the smoke got thicker. The race was temporarily stopped and finally cancelled for the rest of the evening. We didn't know how serious the fire was, but the people there, riders and public, were concerned. The place was packed with kids yelling and screaming.

I think the only ones who were pleased were certain riders who were glad of an early night and were spared the final 26 minutes of the madison. We weren't among them. At the time of the stoppage we were one lap up on our main rivals, Kappes and De Wilde, and they were beginning to crack. In fact Kappes went off the track for a while with 'mechanical' trouble, while De Wilde just rolled around waiting for him. Since they and the Stumpf-Pieters team had more points than us, we needed to press home our advantage in that final session by taking laps.

Monday, 11 November

We learned today that the fire at the track was caused by a cigarette, and that it was the timber frame beneath the banking which was smouldering. There were men working until five the following afternoon to repair it. Whether or not it will affect the outcome of the race, Kappes and De Wilde were certainly back on form tonight.

The racing was highlighted by 45 minutes of live television coverage in *Blick Sport*. Danny sang two songs with the band during the programme, which turned into the Danny Clark Show. The derny race was also shown, but was marred by a serious crash involving Dean Woods and Andreas Klaus, with Klaus being taken unconscious to hospital.

Tuesday 12 November

The good news is that Andreas Klaus is OK after his crash, and was not kept in hospital. When is everyone going to realise the importance of wearing a hard helmet? The pros who train and race for a living should know better.

I was bitterly disappointed not to win the Six, and feel completely deflated. I had really set out to win in Munich. But for the fire, who knows what would have happened on Sunday with the race within our grasp?

Again a full house, and afterwards a meal and a reception were laid on. It was the last thing I felt like, but being a pro I attended. Still, here's to Ghent, and maybe a win in my next Six. Before that it will be nice to get home, if only for a short while.

Result: 1 Andreas Kappes (Ger)/Etienne De Wilde (Bel), 401pts; 2 Stumpf (Ger)/Pieters (Hol), 386pts; 3 Doyle (GB)/Clark (Australia), 246pts at 1 lap

In mid-November, for the first time during the season, the regular riders had to choose between two overlapping events, the Bordeaux 6, which unsurprisingly went to the Frenchmen, Gilbert Duclos-Lassalle and Laurent Biondi, and a shorter event in Vienna which Doyle opted for. This had been introduced as the Night of Vienna, but this year had been stretched to a three-day event, and at some point in the future, if the promoters get their wish, will emerge as a full-blown Six.

VIENNA THREE-DAY

Friday, 15 November–Sunday, 17 November

It seems strange to be racing over just three days and not the full six. Both riders and officials feel lost and somehow lacking in motivation. After Munich there's a sense of anti-climax even if the riders are more relaxed.

Enjoying riding with Stephen Roche, who is good company, but the conditions here are very dangerous. With a lot of road riders on the track – the Italians, Chiappucci and Allocchio, and the local hero, Paul Popp, for instance – you really have to stay alert. At least the accommodation is better than usual as we are staying at the Scandic Crown Hotel 500m from the track, and I am sharing with Danny. The one snag is that all the riders are complaining at having to wait hours for restaurant service.

The crowds have been disappointing but the organisers are really pleased with the racing, and have assured us that the event will continue next year. The city is the main sponsor.

At least we finish early at 5pm on Sunday, so after a mad dash it's possible to leave for home at 6.30pm, with a day to spare before flying on to Brussels on Tuesday morning.

Both Stephen and I were popular with the crowd. It was in Austria, at Villach, that Stephen won his world road race title in 1987, and it was on this Vienna track that I took a silver and bronze medal in the same year. Stephen brought his wife and kids here to round off his final event of the year – 'a holiday on wheels'.

Result: 1 Bruno Holweger/Stefan Joho (Swi); 2 Kappes (Ger)/ De Wilde (Bel); 3 Khrabzov/Ganeev (USSR); 4 Doyle (GB)/Clark (Australia), all on same lap

Doyle and Clark see in the New Year of 1989 at Cologne with their fifth and last joint victory of the season.

Chapter 4

Anthony Adverse

It so happens that Tony Doyle had his first spill on a bicycle three months before he was born. 'It's funny really,' says his mother, Agnes, a great worrier, on her own admission, but a cheerfully enthusiastic talker. 'As I said, I was never a cyclist, but when I was younger I used to go to the shops by bike. One day when I was expecting him – I must have been about six months pregnant – I was riding in Ashford and just as I passed the parish church a Jaguar car door opened and knocked me off. So I often wondered later if what he was doing was going round trying to catch that woman.'

Tony takes some pride – or so he likes to pretend – in having been born in the maternity hospital opposite Hampton Court: 'very prestigious'. So was she, his wife Anne reminds him. 'Well, there you are,' says Doyle. The date was 19 May 1958, the year when Charly Gaul, the Angel of the Mountain, won his only Tour de France and, with more relevance to Doyle's future, Norman Sheil, the first British world amateur pursuit champion, won his second title in Paris.

Tony was the fourth child of a large, close, busy Catholic family who, religion apart, probably owed less to their distant origins in County Wexford than to their immediate London background. His father, Bernard – 'a thoroughgoing cockney', as Tony describes him – and his mother were both from the East End and born within the sound of Bow Bells, at least when the wind was in the right direction. Bernard's father was a conductor with the London Omnibus Company, and had met his mother when she, too, worked on the buses during the First World War. He still regarded himself as Irish, though as a Jewish friend would say to him, 'Call yourself an Irishman, you've never even been to Ireland.' To which Bernard's father could only reply, 'Well, you've never been to Jerusalem.' Agnes remembers him as a man so insistently honest that when a packet of lamb chops was left behind on his bus, he took them round to the police station. Take them home and cook them, they told him.

Bernard was brought up in Poplar, Agnes in Plaistow, where the men of her family had been skilled dockworkers for three generations. 'We share similar social backgrounds – London working class.' The only difference was that, as she puts it, she came from a mixed marriage: her mother was Catholic, while her father, 'a wonderful man, had no religion'. To Bernard and herself, their religion 'has always been very important' – as has the memory of their East End upbringing. 'The London we knew died with the bombing. That killed the heart of it, and that's when we moved away. But the older I get the prouder I am of my roots. The people around us were very basic and hard-working, and we were given a true sense of values.' And those values, which rated people more important than possessions, they did their best, in a matter-of-fact sort of way, to pass on to their children.

There were already two older sisters, Teresa and Janet, and a brother, Philip, when Tony – or Anthony as he always is to the family – arrived. A younger brother, Gerard, was born three and a half years later. The girls had been born in Hendon, but the boys' first home was a semi-detached house at Ashford which, at the whim of the Boundary Commission, has sometimes been in Middlesex and sometimes Surrey. And not far away was an extended family of aunts, uncles and cousins with whom they kept in touch. It was, says Doyle, a crowded and very happy childhood.

Bernard Doyle, who had gone to grammar school and briefly worked as a civil servant before his call-up in the last war, decided to train as a teacher after his demobilisation. When Tony was born he was a schoolmaster at St Michael's, a Catholic primary school around the corner from their home, and by the time Tony was old enough to join his sisters and brother there, his father had been promoted to deputy head and was teaching the final primary year. 'Only Gerard missed out,' says Tony, 'and didn't go through dad's fine tuition', because by then he had moved on to the headship of St Mary's school in Ponders End, North London.

What was it like to be taught by his father? 'It worked out very well. My father was excellent at his job and had a good rapport with the kids. It didn't create any problems at all.' All they had to do was remember to call him Mr Doyle in the classroom, which left several of the other teachers unaware that he was their father. It must have made life easier, too, that Mr Doyle was just as interested in sport as most of his pupils were. He used to organise the football team and run athletics meetings, not just for the school but for the district; he also refereed for the Middlesex Football Association. The only possible disadvantage was that he felt he could never make Philip or Tony the captain of any side.

What Doyle is grateful for is that his father never urged him beyond his natural inclinations at school work:

If you go through teachers' training college and you become a headmaster, you have to be comparatively academic. I mean, he's got the brains, I've got the brawn. But he always recognised how keen I was on sport, and

61

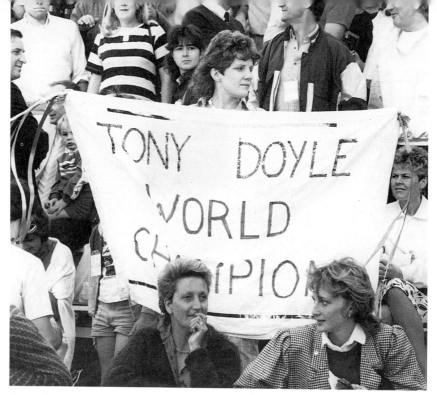

Close family support at Westminster, 1986. Older sister Janet holds up the banner. Younger brother Gerard (top left) and wife, Julie, stand up to be counted

The Paris 6 in 1984, and Tony's mother, Agnes Doyle, who has come over to watch the racing, seems pleased to see that Tony hasn't lost his appetite

Doyle, on a state-of-the-art machine, prepares to leave Buckingham Palace with his father, Bernard, and wife, Anne, after receiving the MBE in 1988

he didn't push me into anything. In fact he let all of us make up our own minds. As long as he saw me doing the right thing he'd be very supportive. Later, when I concentrated on cycling, and it was clear that I intended making that my career, he was wholeheartedly behind me. And I don't think you can ask for anything more, can you?

Doyle describes his mother, too, as protective, loving and caring:

She was very domesticated, and although she had other interests, with five children she obviously found it very difficult to follow them up. Now that the family aren't at home she's got more time to spend on them. She's a keen amateur gardener, which takes her round garden centres and flower shows. She also likes antiques, and has her own antique stall at various fairs.

Agnes describes herself as more a buyer of bric-a-brac and collectables to sell for the Catholic charity, Across, which takes the sick and disabled away on holidays and pilgrimages.

Regular churchgoing was taken for granted, as it still is by Anne and Tony, and all the brothers in turn became altar boys – 'I think they must have heard me singing at the altar, so they didn't ask me to join the choir.'

From St Michael's, Tony went on to Cardinal Godfrey School in Ashford for two years, and then to Salesian College in Chertsey for his third to fifth years. He doesn't recall being at all unhappy at school any more than he was at home. In fact he enjoyed geography and history, though not as much as holidays; and he liked reading at the weekends, though not as much as he does today. But unlike Teresa, who enrolled at teacher training college, and Janet, who went to nursing school, Tony was never going to prolong his education any longer than he had to. At 16 he left school with four O-levels, a steady girl-friend, Anne, a new-found enthusiasm for competing on a bike, and a less than fulfilling clerical job in the Town Hall with the London Borough of Hounslow. Still, he knew that was only a stop-gap until he found something more exciting.

Anne had come into his life at about the same time as cycle racing and in much the same gradual way. She was at the girls' school twinned with his, St John Bosco, and they had known each other since he was 13. Tony's brother, Philip, introduced them on a bus on the way to school. But although Tony noticed her around, especially at school sports days, he was 15 before he met her again at a disco and asked her out to the pictures. They saw *The Sting*, in which, as Tony points out, the man getting stung is called Donegan Doyle. They married six years later and, as one friend put it, this quiet, graceful woman has been 'a girder of strength' during the hard times of his career.

The fact that Tony was smitten by cycling was maybe more surprising. He had been playing football for his school and for the district, and had taken it seriously enough to go for professional trials at Queen's Park Rangers and Fulham. That was in the family tradition: Philip, now a recreational officer with Hounslow Borough Council, was playing football at weekends; so was Gerard, who became a plasterer: 'I think he was distinguished by being sent off the pitch a number of times.' Bernard won't say that he was disappointed by Tony's switch of direction, 'though I suppose I always nourished the idea that he might do something in the football line'.

Cycling was an interest which only Gerard shared. 'He raced for a while in time trials,' says Tony.

Once when he was cycling home from school – he could only have been about 13 at the time – he rode into the back of a stationary car. He was quite badly bashed up, losing all his teeth and having 25 stitches in his head, but it didn't put him off. He was a very good boxer, too, and took part in various amateur tournaments. He still runs regularly, trains in the gym, is extremely fit, and his job, of course, is physically demanding.

Tony was also turning his back on the family's second sport, athletics, at which he had shown some promise. 'When I was eight, nine, ten, my father used to take us all to the White City, where all the major athletics meetings were held at that time. And afterwards we'd queue up to meet the athletes and get their autographs. There was Ron Clarke, he was in his heyday, and Lynn Davies and Lilian Board. They were my heroes then.' Not just starstruck, he became the South Middlesex under-12, under-13 and under-14 champion at 400 and 800 metres, and came fourth in the All-London under-14 cross-country championship. Quite simply, he liked sport of every kind, and being tall for his age without being spindly, and quick on his feet, he succeeded at most of them. He also played cricket for his school and had a county basketball trial.

The cycling more or less crept up on him. As a small boy he had a trike which he pedalled around the garden. Next, when he was about eight, he remembers racing round the block with his brother Philip and some friends on two-wheelers.

Then, when I was about 13, my uncle Pat, who was living in Chiswick, gave me my first adult bike. An all-steel Royal Enfield. I was delighted with it, and when I took it back home I painted it bright orange and fitted steel drop-handlebars on it. Also it had full-rim mudgards, and much to my parents' disgust I cut them down to what I thought were racing mudguards. So there it was, a real pukka racing machine. And that was the first bike on which I could ride around with my friends, and go off exploring during the school holidays.

After that, when I was about 14, I started taking cycling more seriously. Going for longer rides, maybe 30–40 miles – for us that would be an all-day outing. And using the bike more and more to visit friends' houses. Then I started looking at various cycling magazines, and going round the lightweight shops, ogling in their windows. At that time I had a paper round, and even then I had a competitive instinct, because I'd time myself to see how quickly I could cover it. Then I'd do two paper rounds, starting at six and then coming back for another. So I was earning double money, which I spent on bike equipment.

So far this enthusiasm was nothing out of the ordinary. A bike is still the great liberator which separates the youths from the boys, and many get to this stage without ever going on to ride a bicycle in anger. But at 14 and a half Doyle made a move which settled his sporting allegiance for good. He joined his local cycle club, the Clarence Wheelers.

Tony had always been independent and determined, according to his father, and from this point he concentrated on cycling to the exclusion of all his old activities. He trained every evening, raced every Sunday, and Agnes – 'I was always there' – bought one of those slow cookers because she never knew what time he would be back for a meal. And with the children following their separate interests in different places, says Tony, 'my parents couldn't devote themselves to just running me around.' So the club became even more a home from home.

Now with the house and time to themselves Bernard and Agnes, over tea in the front room, describe those early years serenely, as if they were bringing out random verbal snapshots. Bernard: 'Teresa was very good at athletics, and I always hoped she'd do something. But she dropped it at grammar school, and after that I concentrated on the boys ... I remember taking Anthony along to watch Philip play football for the Cubs. The team was short so Anthony said he wanted to play. And he did, in his ordinary shoes, and he put his whole heart into it.' Agnes: 'He always used to take Gerard to school in the morning, and he was very protective of Philip, who had asthma.' Bernard: 'Philip still thinks the world of him. He's convinced he could win the Tour de France if he wanted to.' Agnes: 'Then when they were teenagers, and in and out the whole time, I always said that if I was going to give the house a name it would be Doyle's Doss House.'

Although they had to divide their interests to follow their children's, they would go to watch Tony race whenever they could, especially when he later rode track events like the Champagne and Good Friday meetings at Herne Hill and the national championships in Leicester. His mother went out to Belgium when he was picked for the junior world championships at Liège: 'I found myself a small room above a café, and Tony used to send me off to the market with a list of food he needed. I didn't have any French, but I managed.' She was also in Canada with Bernard when Tony competed in the 1978 Commonwealth Games, and went to visit him in Metz during the first of his two French seasons. The whole family were there to support him when he rode his first Six at Wembley. A winter never passes without some of his brothers and sisters going out to the Continent to watch him race. And of course they all closed ranks around him after his Munich crash. They are, in the words of the wayside pulpit, the family that prays together and stays together.

It is a small coincidence that the first club trip Doyle went on with the Clarence, in November 1972, was to Calshot, near Southampton, where the old Skol six-day track used at Earl's Court in 1967 was now housed in an aircraft hangar. Not a great coincidence, however, since the Clarence had a track racing tradition and Calshot was, and 25 years later remains, the only indoor track in Britain. While too remote to attract commercial racing, it was useful for winter training and the club hired it on a regular basis.

Doyle had never even seen a track before, so obviously he had never seen a pursuit race. All he knew, having been given just five minutes' tuition, was that he was to start from one side of the track and chase another lad who would start from the other. What was supposed to happen then he had no idea, which was unfortunate because he caught his opponent. So what now? Was the race over? Was he to stay behind the other chap until they had completed their ten laps? Or was he to overtake? In which case should he do it on the inside or the outside? All these things were going through his mind, and clearly his opponent was just as inexperienced for he was wobbling all over the place.

At this point Alf Whiteway of the Clarence, who had brought the party down but had gone off on some other business, came back to the track and saw what was happening. 'I thought to myself, oh, no! That's the last person in the world he should be doing a pursuit against. He was the type who is always looking around. I visualised there would be an accident, and that's exactly what happened.' As his opponent veered from side to side, Doyle settled all the questions by running into his rear wheel and falling heavily on the inside of the track.

Doyle takes up the story:

Obviously the club were worried that I'd waste the time they had booked for, so they thought, well, we'll get him out of the way. They carried me down and left me lying on the floor in the changing rooms. They realised that I was a bit shaken up so they gave me a swig out of a hip flask of cherry brandy, and then they carried on training for the next three or four hours. In fact I was in shock, and very uncomfortable because I was badly cut and burnt.

Ghent in 1991 brings Doyle his 23rd six-day victory, here partnered by the local hero Etienne De Wilde. No other British rider has come within sight of this record. At the winners' presentation Pierrot De Wit is holding Tony's nephew and youngest fan, Thomas Langman

When they'd finished they parked me in a car with the bikes and stuff, and one of the parents drove me home. They dropped me off and I managed to stagger up to the front door. And when my mum let me in she couldn't believe it. I was so white, and my arms and legs were cut. They dashed me straight round to Ashford Hospital where they found I had broken my arm. And I also had such severe lacerations on my legs that I ended up coming out of hospital in a wheelchair. So that was my introduction to the sport.

Agnes recalls:

He almost fell in the door – and they'd given him a tot of brandy! A boy of 14! I had to speak to Alf about it. He's a very good man. He's done a lot for Anthony and all his money's gone into the club to help youngsters and keep them on the straight and narrow. But I said, why didn't someone take him to the hospital in Southampton? And he said, well Anthony didn't complain. But he had terrible cuts down his leg. He must have been in agony. I thought that might have put paid to his cycling, but . . .

– she smiles and shrugs.

There was no more racing for a while, but Doyle kept up with the Wheelers' social life, and as the break mended, started going out again on the weekend winter runs. The meet was usually at 9.30 on a Sunday morning at Hampton Court or Shepperton railway station, and from there the crocodile would pedal off for 60–70 miles, stopping just once at a tea-room. It would all pass fairly quietly on the way out, but on the return journey there would usually be a bit of a sort-out as the sparkier members pushed up the pace. Some runs were held as reliability trials, with racing over a set course which the group had to cover in a set time. And after Christmas, as the season approached, the runs would build to around 100 miles, which meant London to Brighton or Worthington and back. But it wasn't all grind: 'You'd be enjoying the countryside as well, and in the early days I went touring and camping with the club.' In fact the Clarence offered most of the diversions of any youth club, since most of the members also met on Wednesday night for darts, table tennis, tea and chat.

Certainly Doyle wasn't in the least deterred by what had happened to him at Calshot. By the end of February 1973 he felt ready – even though his arm was still bandaged up and his wrist was still painful – to ride his first club 10-mile time trial. He knew as little of what was expected of him as he had in the pursuit. He turned up in a Harrington jacket and a pair of Levi jeans and just did what he was he told. But it didn't occur to anyone to explain that this was more than a Sunday morning fun ride.

69

Anthony junior – aka George Doyle born 20 July, 1992

As I saw the other riders coming back along the way I was waving to them and shouting, "All right? How are you?" I didn't know that it was meant to be serious. I didn't have a clue what was involved, and I ended up doing 29-36, which wasn't very good. Of course when I finished the other members came up and asked what was I up to? I was supposed to put my head down and go for it. Anyway, what was I doing riding in a windcheater and trousers when I should have worn shorts and a racing jersey? Luckily I was able to scrounge the right clothes from Alf Whiteway, and the next week I went two and a half minutes quicker. So they were pleased, since I had obviously learnt something. And from there on I was riding the club and the inter-club time trials regularly.

Whatever their feelings about his new preoccupation, his parents never tried to argue him out of it. When I suggested to them that, even allowing for the precarious nature of cycle racing, more than his fair share of spills and other setbacks had come Tony's way, Bernard said, with evident pride: 'A lesser man would have packed up by now.' And even Agnes, who admits that she dreaded him going back on the winter tracks after Munich, simply referred to the hero of a popular pre-war novel who was always getting into and out of scrapes. 'He always reminds me of Anthony Adverse,' she said.

A winter's tale 4

Ghent is the British bikies' home from home. It has three main attractions: it is only an hour's drive from the ferry port of Ostend; it offers an almost inexhaustible supply of local criterium races where apprentices can learn their trade and pros can supplement their earnings; and it is decidedly Anglophile. Among the many British riders to settle there was the late Tom Simpson, whose stay is commemorated by a bronze bust at the entrance to the Sportpaleis where the Ghent 6 is held. It bears the epitaph, *In Memoriam Van Een Groot Gentleman*, and his visiting countrymen regularly leave flowers beneath it. All in all, Ghent is like no other Six, as Doyle explains.

GHENT 6

Tuesday, 19 November

Now have the first night of the Ghent 6 in my legs. Teamed with Etienne De Wilde for only the second time, the other was at Grenoble in 1987 when we finished second.

Ghent is a complete contrast to Munich – it is the working man's Six with antiquated facilities. Noah would feel at home here. All the same it's a Six for the real racing fans, who come for the sport, not the *à la carte* restaurant or the side attractions.

Last night the noise of the student brass band was deafening. The track temperature was tropical (as usual, a case of turn up the heating up and the fans will drink more beer) and not at all comfortable for the riders. It's so dry here, and there's no air to breathe.

Looking forward to the weekend all the same, and the large contingent of British fans who make it a home Six for me. I'm feeling determined and confident, a sure sign. The track here is tight and small, and it was dangerous at the beginning with a few of the riders taking part in their first pro Six. Racing in Ghent keeps your feet on the floor; no chance of becoming pampered or a *prima donna*.

Wednesday, 20 November

The conditions in Ghent are really basic, and the sanitation is dubious, to put it mildly. The airlessness, the heat and noise are getting harder to take. I am sure that the working conditions would not conform to union standards or any Factory Acts. But the secret is to relax and take it all in your stride, to switch off and not let things wear you down. So it's a good job I came prepared with a mobile library and a selection of music for my Walkman.

I can also get well away from the track when I am not racing. This is the one Six where I live not in a hotel or in one of the riders' cabins, but privately in the Brussels home of my soigneur, Pierrot De Wit, and his family.

Thursday, 21 November

Virtually a sell-out tonight and guaranteed sell-out tomorrow. I'm told around 1,500 British fans are expected, and I'm looking forward to that. I am pleased with the way De Wilde and I are racing, always in control and both highly motivated. There was derny racing for the first time tonight, and it will continue for the rest of the Six. It's always popular with the knowledgeable Belgian crowd.

The police are very officious. When it comes to parking at the stadium you would think we were trying to station a tank in front of the Kremlin. Still, Belgian police and Belgian toilets are memorable.

Friday, 22 November

Four days down, two to go. And with this being the fourth Six of the winter, the strain is starting to tell: Bincoletto has retired with stomach trouble, and Khrabzov with saddle sores. A new team of Ganeev and Veggerby has been formed.

Looking forward to racing tonight, and getting ready to loop the loop, with Anne and the family coming over *en masse*. It's amazing how many familiar faces you see from Britain and the Continent; Ghent is a magnet. Lots of champions turned up last night – Peter Post, Wilfred Pefgen, René Pijnen, Walter Planckaert.

The track is not only small – 166m – but very slippery, so you have to be extra careful. Bruno Holenweger crashed and came down last night, but I think the track came off worst. A lot of tired legs in the peloton, which showed how fast and furious the racing had been.

Saturday, 23 November

There they all were: Anne and her sister, Helen, with husband, Mark, and son Thomas, and my sister, Janet. It was good to see them, and luckily De Wilde and I were going well and won the big chase of the evening. Everywhere I turned I seemed to notice a familiar face in the crowd, and it gave me an encouraging feeling.

Another bonus was to stay at the Royal Astrid at Aalst with all the family, particularly as the owner is a bike fan and nothing is too much trouble. A late night, as racing went on until 2.15 am, and we start back on the track at 2.30 in the afternoon for the final day's racing.

Sunday, 24 November

Phew, I can breathe a sigh of relief after my first – or at least my first official – win of the winter. Fantastic support from the crowd, with De Wilde being the local boy and, on my side, so many Brits making the annual pilgrimage from home. A really exciting and thrilling final: even I was getting excited. I was obviously delighted to win, but also pleased to be going so well. It was special with Anne and my sister, Janet, and brother Philip, and brother-in-law, Mark, and his son, Thomas, two and a half, my No 1 and youngest fan.

It was a pleasant change after the race to retire to the luxury of the Royal Astrid and have an enjoyable and relaxing meal with the family and Pierrot. And being dressed in civvies, I almost felt normal.

For once the last night was followed by a leisurely morning, with a 2.55 pm flight to Zurich for the 9 pm start. But if that sounds later than usual, the finish will be later still – 4 am next day. Spent the morning on the phone with journalists and sponsors, and the rest of the time playing with Thomas and relaxing with the family.

Result: 1 Tony Doyle (GB)/Etienne De Wilde (Bel), 484pts; 2 Pieters (Hol)/Tourné (Bel), 470pts; 3 Van Slycke (Bel)/Günther (Ger),

In mid-winter, during a break in the six-day season, Doyle puts in his regular training stint at Herne Hill behind the derny driven, as ever, by Paul Wingrave

Chapter 5

Wheels of chance

Tony Doyle made his own job opportunities. There was no well-worn cycle path to lead him from the Clarence Wheelers into the six-day world. Yet strongly self-motivated as he was, he still owed a lot to chance. He was firmly nudged along the way, for instance, by the fact that the Clarence showed more interest in track racing than the average club; that Herne Hill was within reach of his home at Ashford; and that when he was at his most impressionable age there was a six-day race taking place each year just around the North Circular at Wembley. If he had been brought up in northern England he might never have had the opportunity to ride the track as a boy, and might only have read about six-day racing in the pages of *Cycling*.

Perhaps it wouldn't have made any difference, though. Norwegian Knut Knudsen, an Olympic and world amateur pursuit champion in the early 1970s, came from a country which didn't have a single made-up cycle track to its name. In order to train he would take the ferry across the Skagerrak to Denmark. But he was pretty exceptional. For the most part even ambitious cyclists have been prepared to settle for the types of sport on offer in their own country. And in Britain's case, until half-way through the century, that meant time trialling and point-to-point record making, or racing on shallow Victorian tracks more suitable for pursuiting than sprinting. Massed-start racing was banned from public roads until the 1940s, and since there was no indoor racing either, while the winter track programme was in full swing on the Continent, British cyclists were going through the rigours of the club social season with its annual meetings and dinner dances.

There was a lot to be said for this amateur approach, which created a chummy, good-natured, earnest but essentially decent fraternity of bikies. It provided sport for all ages and levels of competence, an escape from the cities and into the hills, a sort of education in map-reading, mechanics and local geography. And it did so at a price the youngest and poorest could afford. But, comfortable and inward-looking, it was not best suited to produce international champions. And even after British cycling joined the road-racing mainstream of the sport in the late 1940s, much of the old insularity remained. In order to better themselves riders who wanted to make a career of cycling – on road or track – had to move abroad. And to get the full benefit of it, they had to do it young.

The odd thing is that in the early years the development of cycling and cycle racing was just as dynamic in England as in France, even though the French were the prime movers. The first race of all, held over 1,200 metres in the Parc de Cloud in 1868, was won on a Michaux boneshaker, invented seven years before by a Paris firm which normally built perambulators and light carriages. Eighteen months later another Michaux won the first race on the road, from Paris to Rouen, though in this case the iron wheels had been rubber coated to give the bones an easier ride. But in both cases the rider of the winning machine was an Englishman – James Moore, a veterinary surgeon who happened to practise in Paris.

By 1870 the Michaux factory was turning out 400 machines a year, many of which found their way to Britain. Enthusiasts also brought over the next Paris fashion, the penny-farthing. As awkward-looking as a racing camel, and just as hard to handle, it was similarly bred for speed. At a time when pedals were still fixed directly to the front-wheel axle, the bigger that wheel, the more ground it would cover with a single turn of the cranks, and so the faster it would go. Since a machine like this would have cost a working man the equivalent of ten weeks' wages, cycling was not yet a widely popular pastime. But younger members of the middle and upper classes took to it with enthusiasm, enrolled in the riding schools, formed Wheels Clubs and organised musical rides in the parks.

In 1839 a Scottish blacksmith, Kirkpatrick Macmillan, had anticipated the Michaux family by 22 years with a more sophisticated form of bicycle than the boneshaker. Instead of pedals to be pushed around, it had treadles which were pressed up and down with the feet. These turned the back wheel by a series of cranks. But the Macmillan wasn't taken up commercially, and it was only in the mid-1870s that Britain's industry, which took a proper pride in its engineering skill and inventiveness, began to make significant changes to the basic design of the bicycle. The days of the precarious penny-farthing, weighing up to 50lb and at the mercy of every pothole and cross-wind, were numbered. The search was on for a practicable bicycle with more closely matching wheels – halfpenny-farthing if not halfpenny-halfpenny – and some means of transmitting pedal power to the wheel at the rear.

After several worthy efforts by others, James Starley of Coventry finally cracked it in the mid-1880s with his Rover safety model. It had a diamond frame, a continuous chain drive from pedals below the saddle, and wheels of equal size. In essence it was the machine that most people ride today. This advance instantly made the bicycle less outlandish in appearance and more attractive to ride – though not instantly low-priced. That would only come with mass production. But by 1896 there were as many as 700 British factories turning out variations on the same idea, and with French industry still suffering from the effects of the Franco-Prussian war, Coventry had become the world capital of cycle-making.

Cycling was well established, both as a recreation and a sport, before these developments. Because people found it more convenient to travel by rail than by road, British roads outside the towns had become badly neglected towards the end of the nineteenth century. They were rough, rutted, muddy and frequently fouled by horses. But this did not deter the intrepid members of the Cyclists' Touring Club, which was founded in 1878 and reached a membership peak of over 60,000 in 1899. At least they faced little opposition from the motor car, which was not allowed on the public roads until 1896 or to exceed 12mph until 1903. But the same speed limit also applied to cycles, and since there were frequent prosecutions for 'furious riding', the most that enthusiasts could hope to get away with was solitary attempts at distance and place-to-place records.

For straightforward racing they needed a better surface and a private place in which they would be free from interference by the police. And so the first professional events, which began in 1871 and usually took the form of challenge matches over anything from one to ten miles, were held on paths in enclosed areas like the Star Grounds in Fulham or the Aston Cross Grounds in Birmingham. They proved so popular that circuits of ash, ash and battens, shale, gravel and grass were prepared, and after 1891, when the first cement track was laid at Putney, many took up the same idea.

The races were carefully orchestrated. The organisers first put in solo riders to stir up the action in the opening laps. Later they introduced tandems to set the pace, and finding that this went down well with the spectators they progressed to building up the speed of the pacing by bringing in multiple cycles from triplets through quads and quints to ten-man 'dectets'. To advertise their products, Dunlop at one period in the 1890s deployed a team of 60 pacemakers, taking on extra men for big events. Cycle-makers like Humber, Rudge and Swift sponsored the riders who raced behind them. And crowds of up to 15,000 turned up at Herne Hill and Paddington to bet on the results with the trackside bookies.

Then, as rapidly as the cycling craze had flared up in the last decade of the nineteenth century, so it died down in the first decade of the twentieth. The car arrived to lure away the better-off patrons, and in 15 years the membership of the CTC slumped by 52,000 to only 8,000 by the outbreak of the First World War. The industry, which anyway had been over-producing, found the bottom had dropped out of their market. Most of the professional riders, in turn, were forced out of business through lack of sponsors, and the track meetings lost their old appeal.

Amateur track racing continued. Indeed, it went through its most suc-cessful phase ever with Leon Meredith winning seven world championship gold medals as a stayer, and W J (Bill) Bailey four as a sprinter in the period 1904–13. In 1968, at the age of 80, Bailey was living in Bedford Park, the first of the London garden suburbs, a tall, handsome man, with a glass of sherry for any visitors and an almost total recall of his pre-war years. 'Oh, there was Ben Jones, he could go a bit,' he'd muse. 'And Vic Johnson and Leon Meredith and Ernie Payne and Clarence Kingsbury. Oh, there were lots of us at that time.' He was surprised to find himself in their company, since (like Doyle) he was more of a footballer: 'I'd won the first two races on the new White City track, but I hadn't much other experience. Still I was strong, and I suppose they put me in for good measure.'

The professional era had left the amateurs with some good tracks like Herne Hill and Crystal Palace. But most of the others were made of cinders and laid almost flat; some were still just plain grass. And certainly he and the others had seen nothing like the high-bank velodrome at Copenhagen where the 1909 world championships were staged: he won. And again in Brussels, Rome and Berlin, missing only the 1912 championships in the USA because the National Cyclists' Union couldn't raise the fare. In 1914 he turned professional and after the war rode successfully, though never again invincibly, in America and all over Europe. Afterwards he went into the cycle industry and started a cycle magazine. There wouldn't be another English sprinter like him, or a golden era like his, until Reg Harris came to the top just before and after the next world war.

Cycling didn't disappear meanwhile, it simply changed character and, as far as the sporting side was concerned, tried to make itself invisible. From being a luxury worth affording for its pace and social chic, the bicycle became a necessity on which the grocer's boy ran his errands, the policeman did his rounds and the housewife her shopping. Every mine and factory had its bicycle stands and shelters. But it still had the capacity to thrill simply by obeying the rider's muscles and transporting him where no bus or train would take him – as was evident from the number of chain gangs threading their way over the Pennines on weekends and summer evenings. The for-tunes of the bicycle revived, and in 1939 CTC [Cyclists' Training Club] membership, always a good barometer of public interest, had picked up to 36,000.

The bicycle, too, was still a racing machine, even if the style of racing in Britain was very different from that on the Continent. Time trialling was introduced by F T Bidlake of the North Road club in 1890s in the hope of avoiding the attention of the police. The National Cyclists' Union, under pressure from the authorities, had already banned massed start racing, and the North Road responded by holding its 24-hour road race on the track. But the riders missed the atmosphere of the open road, and the event was

77

not a success with them or with the public. So Bidlake's idea was to return to the highway, but to send single riders off at intervals to cover the course, reckoning that if they were riding normal bikes and dressed in normal clothes they would pass unnoticed.

The first time trial was held in October 1895 over 50 miles, and to ensure that the riders didn't end up in clusters on the road, pacing was strictly forbidden. In poor weather only 6 of the 22 starters finished, but Bidlake thought the experiment worth repeating. The NCU specifically added time trials to their banned list two years later, but the activity spread and on the whole came to be tolerated by the police provided that the riders respected the general rules of the road.

So, after the turn of the century, when the classic one-day races and the Tour de France were being established and trying to drum up all the publicity they could, the British adopted a form of cycle racing, based on secrecy and discretion, which went to the other extreme. Even after it had set up a governing body in 1922 – which later adopted its present name, the Road Time Trials Council – it remained so anxious to avoid creating waves that it forbade any prior notice of events, referred to its courses by a code number, and started in the early hours in order to finish before other road users were up and about. Bicycles had to carry bells, and the 'inconspicuous clothing' rule stipulated black tights and black jackets long after changes in fashion had made them glaringly obvious. It was 1950 before contestants were allowed to wear club jerseys.

It's tempting to mock the growing conservatism of a body which had started out as thoroughly subversive. But what time trialling did was keep competition on the British roads alive, and give a sporting purpose to cycle clubs which would otherwise have been purely recreational.

Like the NCU, the RTTC was opposed to massed-start racing, afraid that it might provoke legislation which would interfere with its own activities. But a new rebel organisation, the British League of Racing Cyclists, was set up to promote it. Even before the war, racing had been staged by enthusiasts on the motor circuit at Brooklands, and in 1942 the BLRC decided to test official reaction by putting on a race along public roads between Wolverhampton and Llangollen. The skies did not fall in. And although it was many years before grudging acceptance of road racing gave way to cheerful police cooperation, by the time Tony Doyle was born in 1958 the Tour of Britain was in its sixth year and just about to become the Milk Race. And by the time he took up cycling 14 years later, there was little an English rider couldn't do if he had the talent and the mind to do it.

Besançon 1980: world pro pursuit champion only weeks after failing to get a ride at the Moscow Olympics. Left to right: Herman Ponsteen, silver; Doyle, gold; Hans Oersted, bronze

Colarado Springs 1986. Six years after his victory at Besançon, Doyle is back in the rainbow jersey, having got the better of his constant rival, Oersted (left). On the right, with the bronze, is the Dane, Jesper Worre

A winter's tale 5

The Zurich 6, the only one staged in Switzerland, was first run in 1954 and yet in many ways is a throwback to the hard-riding pre-war era. It prides itself on having the strictest discipline and the longest working day on the circuit. Its director, Joseph Voegli, insists that the racing continues until the city's public transport start up the following morning. But while this may help to keep a hard core of hard-drinking spectators off the streets, it also keeps the riders in the saddle for what increasingly seems to them an unreasonably hard night-shift.

ZURICH 6

Monday, 25 November

Having completed the first night's racing here you realise that it's going to be a really long week – from 8 pm to 4 am each day. We must be out of our minds. The last couple of hours really drag, as the crowd has left and we racing in front of only a couple of hundred people – and most of those are drunk. You don't have to be mad to race in Zurich, but it sure helps.

The one relief is that the promoter now lets us stay in a hotel instead of in a caravan in the car park. He must be going soft.

At least I kept up my momentum from Ghent by winning the opening chase and taking the overall lead with my partner, Stan Tourné. Every year we say, Zurich, never again.

Tuesday, 26 November

No rest for the wicked. There was never a truer word spoken, for after finishing at 4 am we were back on the track at 2 pm for an afternoon session in front of a couple of thousand kids. Long nights and long days. They treat you better when you are serving time. We all wonder what we are doing when we trudge the kilometre back to the hotel at 4.45 in the morning. We wonder if Becker and Lendl would ever do the same.

We were kept entertained in the early hours by a couple of gorgeous transvestites in the back straight, who became the butt of all the jokes. They really enjoyed all the attention that 34 pro bike riders were giving them. It makes a change from the normal drunks who are left in the stand at that time of the morning.

Wednesday, 27 November

Trapeze artistes, knife throwers, stunt motorcyclists, singers and yodellers all combined to make the Gala Night. A hard day's work with another 2–4.30 afternoon session, and then the 7.45 pm–4.0 am 'evening' session with a 100-minute madison.

Beer sales must have been good because the crowd seemed really happy and stayed on for a long time. As we descended to the massage cabins in the bowels of the hall, we felt like coal miners coming off the night-shift.

Thursday, 28 November

Tonight the racing was really hard, long and fast, with a 100km madison. I was struggling early on but got better and better as the race continued. Towards the end I was flying. There was a good crowd because the 100km chase attracts the real fans.

Tourné and I ended up in second place behind the Swiss pair, Joho and Stutz, just missing out on points in the three sprints at the end of the chase. Stan is really suffering from crutch trouble, and I am wondering whether he will be able to finish the event.

Friday, 29 November

Friday night brings a bigger crowd with the 75km handicap. A lot of the riders are feeling handicapped by a stomach bug which is floating around. Toilet paper is at a premium.

Just in case we aren't feeling tired enough, the racing is now until 5.0 am.

The Swiss new boys, Bruno Risi and Kurt Betschart are riding really well in their home Six – only the second they have ever ridden – and are the finds of the winter. They have a great future.

Saturday, 30 November

It's a nice feeling to be going home, even if it is directly after the finish. Yet again we raced 8 pm–5 am, followed by a mad dash to get paid and packed, then pay the personnel, and finally rush to the airport to catch the first plane out to London at 7.30. I am looking forward to sleeping in my own bed. And after 35 days of competition out of 39 I am going to let my hair down when I get home and have a traditional English breakfast. The thought of it has kept me going today.

Everyone was very tired, and a lot of riders were going down with colds and stomach upsets. Still I finished. Another Six under my belt.

Result: 1 Werner Stutz/Stefan Joho (Swi), 323pts; 2 De Wilde (Bel)/ Holenweger (Swi), 307pts; 3 Risi/Betschart (Swi), 263pts, at 1 lap; 6 Doyle (GB)/Tourné (Bel), 51pts, at 5 laps

Chapter 6

Alf Whiteway of the Clarence

The cycling club which Doyle joined in December 1972, the Clarence Wheelers, had, like his Hampton Court birthplace, a misleadingly regal ring to it: Clarence, the ducal title given to younger sons of the royal family; Clarence House, home of the Queen Mother. You would at least imagine that the club had been founded in the early years of the century when royal Christian names – Albert, Edward, George – were all the rage, and the great time-trialling clubs were ... well, a bit socially exclusive. The Clarence, in fact, was formed in 1934 by a 22-year-old butcher's errand boy, Alf Whiteway, and its first members were 13 other errand boys. It took the name Clarence because that was the name of the square in Teddington, with the Clarence Hotel on the corner, where the lads used to gather before setting out on their Sunday jaunts into the country.

Alf Whiteway, now in his early 80s, is one of those living advertisements for the benefits of regular cycling on what remains of the open road and of a single all-absorbing interest. They are clearly what have kept him going. It has not been a charmed life. He had a bad accident in 1986, when he was hit by a car as he rode home from a club meeting, and he has also suffered two strokes. But with a stubborn need to get back into action, he has managed to minimise the effects of both. He remains an active life president of the Clarence – Doyle himself is chairman – and the guardian of its founding idea of mutual help and encouragement.

Alf Whiteway lives in the house in which he grew up, a small, semi-detached cottage behind the main road in Hampton Hill, and we talked in a front room apparently cluttered with spare bicycle parts, programmes, entry forms and memorabilia largely relating to Doyle, his most successful protégé. I say apparently, because all these items turned out to be arranged so that they were within easy reach of his chair and telephone. We were twice interrupted, first by a well-known rider who rang up for details of the

Alf Whiteway of the Clarence Wheelers smiles for the camera in 1974 before presenting Anthony Doyle with the trophy for a 10-mile time trial

At the age of 16 Doyle, here riding an early-season trial, already has his eyes fixed on a career in cycling

time trial course being used the following Sunday, which Whiteway reeled off, rehearsing, in the way old bikies have, every roundabout and landmark, bend, slope and road number. Next a junior member of the club called at the door to borrow a pair of pedal cranks. Whiteway fished them out and handed them over with no more than a 'Just remember where they came from, won't you?'

He always seems to have been a man of some consequence, and remembers his early days in lengthy monologues which have an engaging touch of vanity. He was never short of self-confidence.

When I worked for a butcher, I was so good at salesmanship that the manager of the shop had to keep splitting up my round. It was getting too big. I was putting on new customers too fast. Mind you, as a young man I suppose I could say I was more appealing to the customers. I had long wavy hair and I suppose I was good-looking. I always had a cheerful disposition about myself, and I was very popular with them because I could talk butchering. And that was because I learnt it.

I had been at the butcher's shop about a fortnight and never asked any questions about how to do this and that, just watched how it was being done. And one day the old boy who was an assistant there, and used to work down the bottom of the yard cutting up the meat, was called up to the shop because they were busy. There was a forequarter of beef lying on the table, waiting to be cut, and I got the knife and cut it up into the respective joints. When this chap came back he said, who did that? I said, I did. Who taught you that? Nobody, I said, I watched how you did it. He said, you done that excellent. You can always do it in future now. So that was the beginning of cutting up meat, and learning how to do things.

How I got that job, by the way, was by seeing an advert in the shop window and walking in for an interview. And the owner there was an Australian, and he went back to Australia. Probably about 25 years later, his son was in England. He came round to see me and asked me to go back to Australia with him. He needed my help. They valued my services, you see. But of course mother was a widow, there was a family of four, and I was the person who was fetching in money, which was badly needed. So I never got permission to go. I stayed in dear old English.

And instead devoted himself to the Clarence Wheelers.

In the 1930s every High Street shop made home deliveries, and errand

Teeth clenched and on his way to victory in the 1983 Kellogg's city centre race at Nottingham

boys on their heavy, gearless bikes, with big wicker baskets on the front, were the kings of the road, the lads who whistled through the traffic and sped down the hills no hands. They would all meet each other on their daily rounds, and it's not surprising that 14 of them should band together for busmen's holidays at the weekends. But it must have needed all the breezy assurance of Whiteway, still a teenager when it all began, to turn these unprivileged casuals into one of the most successful clubs in the south-east. 'I was the leader of that group. Wherever we went I used to plan it, and we really enjoyed ourselves. We absolutely lived for Sundays to get out on the bicycle.' In the face of Whiteway's driving enthusiasm, the others probably never stood a chance of lying in on a Sunday.

Although Whiteway had already formed the idea of turning the group into a recognised club, which raced as well as rambled on two wheels, it took him five years to accomplish. 'We made attempt after attempt. We were 14 complete novices, myself as well, and this game of racing was completely new. We had to learn it. We had to get affiliated to the Road Time Trials Council and the National Cycling Union. I always felt that someone's got to take the initiative.'

The regulars finally decided where and when the club would meet, where it would race, and what it would be called: 'The name Clarence Wheelers Cycling Club was proposed incidentally by myself.' And he proposed it not simply because that was their mustering station on Sunday morning, but to avoid giving the club a district title which might have put off cyclists from further afield. So now, with all the formalities completed, the Clarence was officially founded in February 1934.

From that day it has never looked back. By 1935 we were promoting our first race [a time trial, naturally, not a massed-start race] on the Portsmouth Road. We were in the London South District Council then, now it's London West. And that first race was a success. I'm trying to remember the name of the timekeeper, a person well known in the Tooting Bicycle Club. That's it, Dixie Dean, a very good man.

Having its events officially accepted didn't mean neglecting the old weekend outings through the Home Counties and down to the coast while the going was still good. Cycle touring, like organised hiking and scouting and other bids to escape from the cities, were at their height of popularity in the 1930s, and, says Whiteway,

Dressed to kill. In December 1991 Moscow stages its first six-day race, and in Red Square sporting a Red Army hat Doyle poses before the onion domes of St Basil's, the cathedral built by Ivan the Terrible

The Clarence was considered to be one of the best social types of club in the district. I was the captain, and I used to lead a run with 20 riders practically every Sunday. We would go out into the country, visit places, stop for refreshments. Sometimes we would have four or five girls with us. Mostly youngsters, but they'd cover a good mileage, and they were very happy with the day's outing. Even on the way back they'd be looking forward to the next time and asking me where we'd going.

I took to that sort of thing, studied maps, knew where the east was, and the north, west and south, and never worried if I got lost momentarily in the country. I knew roughly the lie of the land, where the hills were. ... We also had an attic at the back of a greengrocer's shop in the High Street, Teddington, where we met one evening in the week. We used to have some fun, we really did, we enjoyed our company. And that's what cycling was all about.

The scene of the fun was eventually moved from the attic to the Jolly Masons in Walpole Road, Teddington, where the first split came, some 30 members breaking away to start the Teddington Cycling Club – 'but it only lasted three years'. And there was another rendezvous on Sunday night, the City Arms, Long Ditton, where several clubs finished their runs. 'On a good night you could count as many as 70 riders there.' Now the Clarence meets on a Tuesday evening at the hut of the third Hanworth Scout Group. Of the current 90 members about 27 turn up. 'There have been times when we have been struggling a bit, but we've always progressed. Any youngster who came into the club and hadn't quite got the right bicycle for the purpose, he was helped, mostly by myself. Or if not by me, by somebody else in the club.'

It was soon after the Second World War that the Clarence reached its peak membership, 110, and began to make a national name for itself as a racing club. And this spread even further in the 1950s when two of its best time triallists, Mike Gambrill and Alan Killick, also developed into highly successful trackmen. Gambrill rode in the team pursuit at the 1956 Olympics and together they set a 30-mile tandem record which stood for a quarter of a century. As is the way, their successes attracted other ambitious young riders. 'It was once overheard by me, at one of the open races, two individuals commenting on all the Clarence riders on the start sheet. One of them remarked, 'Oh, the Clarence have got this wrapped up. They'll probably have the winner, maybe the second, third and fourth, and take the team as well. And that was generally true at that time.'

One reason that Gambrill and Killick took so naturally to track racing was that they were already, at Whiteway's insistence, riding track bikes with fixed wheels on the road. He was convinced that no aspiring rider should be allowed to ride with variable gears until he had mastered turning a fixed wheel. And he had both the strength of opinion and the cash to insist on this in the club. During the war he had left butchering and become an army cook, and after it was over he was earning what he describes as good money as a chef at the Shepperton film studios. Being unmarried, living simply and having few other interests, he was able to devote a great deal of that money to the Clarence. It was he who had the idea of putting Gambrill and Killick on a tandem, and he who paid for it. He has a soft spot for tandem racing, and even now owns four machines, two of them in use, one waiting for suitable enthusiasts to ride it, and the fourth in need of renovation.

I had about 26 track bikes of my own which I bought from different people at different times, and I loaned them out to members of the club, particularly youngsters. I'd put them in the right gear, and then they were for riding on the road to get used to the art of pedalling. I've always maintained that what youngsters need is rhythm in their pedalling. Once they've got rhythm they can do almost anything.

As far as Doyle remembers, he turned up with just one other lad to join the Clarence, but Whiteway's circumstantial account of his first appearance also has some ring of truth to it.

He came along with three others, and I think that in the end two of them joined. It's the usual practice. A group of youngsters think they're going to take up cycling and join a club. So one is braver than the others, and he takes the initiative and puts the question. Immediately I spotted in Tony a person that was going to do something, a person that's got talent. He was determined, and always clear in his intentions.

He came along with his bicycle. It was not up to club standard, so I gave him a track bike to get used to. And he lived on that bicycle. He took to the sport like a duck to water.

Although Doyle's debut at Calshot had been inauspicious, and his first time trial had caused the wrong kind of stir, his second impressed Whiteway considerably:

He was still in trouble after the accident, and riding holding the tops of the bars because he couldn't get down to the bends. But he still did the fastest time out of 17 riders in the event. The others were talking about it afterwards. They were amazed that he was only 14 and a half.

All this was new to him, but we soon got him into the way of doing things. And he was one of those individuals who, every time he rode, he knocked time off. He kept improving. And that's how it went on, week after week. He was so determined even when things went against him. It was the same when I put him on a tandem a few years later. The pair of them were on the Hampton course, and as they had turned and got back to the war memorial, they punctured. But it didn't deter Tony. He rode that tandem to the finish with a flat tyre, keeping it upright for a 22 min ride. I thought that was extraordinarily good.

As time went by I realised Tony's potential, so I would sort out races for him. Tony would come here and stay overnight if we were going out early Sunday morning. Fortunately I had a person called Derek Taplin who was very good at taking us around. We would leave at 4.30 or five o'clock in the morning, according to where the race was. We would take Tony and Tony would perform. Sometimes we'd go as far as Oxford or into Essex or down the New Forest area. We once went all the way up to Cleveland, near Tyneside, for the national championship 25.

At this stage it was always time trials, never road races, of which he was highly suspicious, though he denies that he has any basic prejudice against them. 'I have been to some road races and watched them, and it's my opinion that the way they are conducted in this country, we will never ever have a world road race champion. There is too much sitting in, too much blocking. None of those things I agree with. But I've never tried to talk people out of doing road racing. It's just in my nature to talk time trialling all the time.'

It clearly meant a lot to Whiteway, who had given his life to the Clarence, to discover and advise a rider who would go that much further than Gambrill and Killick had been able to do. And more than that, a rider who would always acknowledge his debt to Alf and the club. And this Doyle does genuinely. He is grateful to Whiteway not only for practical help and support, but for grooming him into the Clarence 'way of doing things' – that mixture of fixed wheels, time trialling and track racing, which he now believes is the best introduction he could have had to the sport.

When you start off riding a single fixed wheel [first it was 69–70in then 73in], you've got to pedal when you go downhill. Nowadays youngsters have got a 16-speed bike with a 12-up block, and they shove it into the top gear and go whacking down that hill. That's good fun, but they really shouldn't have the type of gear that professionals use in the Tour de France. They should be restricting themselves, learning what the French call *souplesse*. Because while you can pedal your way out of trouble, you can't always push your way out. You find it very hard and you are labouring. Sometimes in a big gear you just grind to a stop.

If riders have a long career, I put that down to the fact that they are pedallers, because pushing a big gear puts more pressure on the joints of the body. Take Joop Zoetemelk, who won a world road race championship at 38 – that was in Italy in 1985. Now he was renowned for being a pedaller. When he used to wear out a sprocket on his bike, it wasn't the 13 or 14 sprocket, it was the 17 because he spent more time in that than any other. And one reason why six-day riders carry on longer in their careers is that they are pedalling with a lower gear. They traditionally use a gear of 52-16, which is 87.7in.

As far back as September 1980, when Doyle had been a professional for less than a month and was competing in the world pursuit championships at Besan, the shrewd cycling rider, J B Wadley, described him as 'one of the fastest pedallers in the world'. And after Doyle had won the title, he noted: 'Doyle is a strapping 6ft 1in lad, strong enough to use the biggest of gears, but he always chooses a combination of chairwheel and rear fixed sprocket below the average. During his four winning rides he selected 53 and 16, or 89in. In a one-off race the advantage is with the big-gear man, but Doyle weathered four hard rides in two days better than his rivals.' It was a compliment to Doyle which Whiteway, too, was entitled to share. Doyle explains:

Higher gears have become fashionable because we've now got the 12-tooth back sprocket. And so the Continentals who use them are going faster. But lads here who ride stretches of dual carriageway in time trials are using a 12-tooth sprocket with a 55, 56, 57-tooth chainwheel. Over there they would never do that. They might use a 12-tooth sprocket, but with a 52 or 53. And they will be going at 55–60 kilometres an hour, which is 35–37mph, while here they won't be doing much above 20mph.

If Doyle had come later onto the scene and had joined another club, he too might have adopted a different set of heroes and become an out-and-out tester. He might even have stuck to that peculiarly English speciality. Fortunately he had a more liberal cycling education which gradually introduced him to the track and put no obstacles in his way when eventually he felt that, to develop his all-round ability, he needed to branch out into road racing.

He still feels that the kind of time trialling practised by the Clarence provided the best introduction to the sport he could have had – 'far better than being pitched straight into road racing or onto the track. As a schoolboy you can ride at your own speed in a time trial without the risk of bringing off other riders. You can find your own way into the sport. I know the years I spent mainly doing that stood me in good stead.'

At first the track was just a diversion. The club would go over to train at Herne Hill, the shallow asphalt bowl, 457m round, which had been built before the turn of the century. There Whiteway would coach them in the rudiments of racing, and they would hold club championships. But Doyle was 16 before he first competed seriously on the track, in the Easter meeting at Portsmouth in 1975.

Within a couple of years the Clarence would no longer be the centre of his cycling activities. He would become a part of the national squad system and absorbed in training sessions aimed at international events. But even as a professional he has kept in touch with the club. He helps the younger riders, goes to the social evenings when he can, attends committee meetings, and half a dozen times a year he give talks to his own and other clubs on training, diet and equipment. The Clarence in turn arranges its annual dinner for February, after the six-day season is over, just to make sure that he will be free.

'A lot of money was spent on Tony,' says Whiteway.

It had to be because the talent was there. He had to have all the things that were needed. But he's never forgotten that, for every so often he'd chuck me over fifty or so in appreciation for what I'd done, and he's always thought of me. When I had a stroke on Christmas night, 1990, and was in hospital for three months, he used to come and visit me every other day. He's been a great asset to us, and he still is.

To someone like Doyle, the benefit of this continued involvement still cuts both ways.

It helps you keep your feet on the floor. The classic example is the Zurich 6, which comes at the end of a bout of half-a-dozen Sixes, and finishes at six o'clock on the Sunday morning. I always change quickly and dash to the airport to catch the early plane, get home, have breakfast and go to bed. You're dog-tired and all you want is sleep. But the word will have got round that I'm home and that the Sixes are over for a short spell. And you can be sure that someone will have phoned Anne to let her know that there's a club run starting at 9.30 that morning. Just so I'm aware. It's the high spot of the week to them. And they can't quite understand why it isn't the same for me.

A winter's tale 6

There was no open display of grief among the riders gathered at Zurich when it was rumoured that the Moscow 6, already postponed from October, was likely to be scuppered once more, this time by visa problems. But contracts are there to be honoured, and once the red tape had been disentangled, instead of breaking up early for Christmas they headed east for the most bizarre event of their season.

The Six was a German initiative, organised by Frank Minder, director of the Bremen 6, and sponsored by Beck's Beer and Siemens, the electronics company. The most remarkable thing about the event was that it took place at all. It was staged at Krylatskoye, the 1980 Olympic velodrome built out in the Moscow suburbs beyond the ring road. This is a stadium of now-fading grandeur, too large and remote to be ideal for six-day racing, and difficult to reach from the centre, especially in several inches of snow. Attendances rarely exceeded 3,000.

For Doyle, though, the visit had a particular significance. It was at Krylatskoye 11 years before that he had ridden his last amateur race: the Olympic team pursuit. Moscow had been the pivot of his cycling career.

MOSCOW 6

Wednesday, 4 December

It feels as though we are going on a school trip, but it's a funny sort of trip — to Moscow. After leaving Heathrow at 7.55 am I flew to Frankfurt where all the riders and personnel assembled, and then on to Moscow with the rest. There was chaos checking all the bikes, dernys and luggage, and the flight was delayed three hours. Eventually we arrived at the track, and were given rooms there which turned out to be disgusting, filthy, stinking and full of cockroaches. The curtains were thin and didn't meet in the middle, which would make it almost impossible to sleep on in the morning.

So we complained and demanded the hotel we had been promised. But after waiting up until 1.30 am, we were told that it wasn't possible and we would have to stay at the track, though only for the first night. We had to accept this, though two of the German riders, who found blood on their dirty bed linen, preferred to move chairs out into the corridor and sleep on these.

The Soviet national squad uses these rooms when they come here to train, but though they may seem paradise to them, to us they were pure hell.

Thursday, 5 December

This was the opening of the Six, and chaos reigned supreme both on and off the track. Jens Veggerby, who had the next room to Danny's and mine, claims to have killed 89 cockroaches. But tonight our accommodation has been switched to a military hostel, it's cleaner but uncomfortable.

We are not too happy, either, with the racing, which has been dangerous because of the steepness and slipperiness of the track. While training in the afternoon I slid down the full height of the banking, suffering bruises and minor cuts. And when the programme began the inexperience of the Russian riders added to the risks. The speaker and the crowd could not understand the racing, the electronic scoreboard gave hardly any information, and everyone was wondering what was going on.

Friday, 6 December

After one night at the military hotel we were transferred to the International Tourist hotel, an improvement though still pretty basic. Then after a short rest we were ferried back to the track by bus.

Danny and I were riding effectively together and won the madison event, but the two Russians, Khrabzov and Ganeev, with their higher points total from the sprints and devils and so on, took the lead in the Six. Every 100pts counts as a lap, and they are both sprinting very well.

You really need to stay alert as some of the riders are pretty dodgy and tonight four riders hit the deck. It is very chilly on the track, and after sitting around for a long time it is very difficult with cold legs to step straight into it. The derny racing is proving very popular with the crowd.

Saturday, 7 December

An eventful day, with the temperature down to -15°. First a visit to the Kremlin and Red Square followed by lunch in Hotel Russia. And then Saturday night brought a crowd of 6,000 to the track and made for a much better atmosphere. It is all very new for the crowd, a real learning process.

Because the riding has been so dangerous, with numerous crashes, the organisers decided not to have any madisons tonight. A six-day without chases. Whatever next? So the teams are being separated by points, which is an advantage to Khrabzov and Ganeev, who are continuing to sprint well to maintain their lead.

The highlight of the evening was Remig Stumpf attempting to drive the bus back to the hotel. We were all in fits until a rear axle broke. We eventually changed buses, but Remig was worried about how the police and military were going to react.

Sunday, 8 December

The Six seems strange. Just because it's the first in Moscow? Or is it the size of the track – 333.33m, the biggest indoor Six ever? Or the absence of the madison? Sprinting legs have now become essential, and because 100pts equals one lap, Khrabzov and Ganeev are now leading by two laps from Bincoletto and Veggerby in second place with Danny and me third. The track doesn't give the impression of speed, maybe because it is so big and cold.

At last I have been able to telephone home without too many problems. Thank heavens for credit card phones. It was also a wise choice to bring our own chef, food and kitchen staff – the Germans who organise the catering at the majority of Sixes.

Monday, 9 December

One day to go. The talk is that the Moscow 6 will be held again next year. The organisers think that, in spite of the problems, it has a future here. Khrabzov and Ganeev have kept their two-lap lead, and look unstoppable now with no chases to give the others a chance of reining them in. It really goes against the grain of six-day racing. The other leading positions are still the same.

I hope that we will have a large crowd for the final night. One problem is that there are no printed programmes for the public. I am sure it would help the public to understand the racing and identify the riders if there was something available to explain the pairings, the rules, the history of the Sixes, and so on.

Tuesday, 10 December

All credit to the organisers for managing to pull off this Six – the first in Moscow and the first pro Six to have Russian winners – in view of the uncertainty and the political upheaval. It made me realise the extent of the problems that the average Muscovites face. And it made me appreciate things at home much more. It was nice to get the race under my belt, and now I am really looking forward to a ten-day break in Florida and seeing some sun. From -15°C to +20°C, quite a change.

Result: 1 Konstantin Khrabzov/Marat Ganeev (USSR), 458pts; 2 Bincoletto (It)/Veggerby (Den), 381pts, at 2 laps; 3 Clark (Australia)/Doyle (GB), 291pts, at 2 laps

Chapter 7

Trial runs

There's no doubt that Doyle was something of a prodigy. When the Clarence Wheelers held their 40th annual dinner at the end of his novice season, this tall 15-year-old schoolboy with long, floppy brown hair had 24 trophies and 36 medals on display in the dining room of the Excelsior Hotel in West Drayton. They included the prizes for 6 club records and 10 championships. The popular Vin Denson, former Tour de France rider and guest of honour, recalled the tussles he'd had with Mick Gambrill and Alan Killick in the mid-1950s, and wasn't the only one in the room to wonder if the good old days in the history of the Clarence weren't returning. In the last year the club had attracted 24 riders under the age of 17, captained by Doyle. Alf Whiteway, their president, never one to sell his protégé short, commended Doyle for his 'leadership, guts, determination and will to succeed. While we have this situation then we need not fear the next 40 years.'

The 1974 season, which brought Doyle's 16th birthday and promotion from schoolboy to junior, continued in much the same style: constant time trialling and regular success. He won three bottles of sherry in as many events over Easter, his club's annual Bennett Memorial 25 for a solid silver cup inscribed with the names of Gambrill and Killick, and on a happier return to Calshot, the Wheelers' indoor championship. Of the 51 events he rode, he won 25, breaking another 6 club records and taking 5 more titles. He also confided to a local paper that he had set his sights on the next but one Olympics. But Whiteway, in the role of best friend and sternest critic, seemed anxious to make sure he didn't become complacent, for in his speech at the following annual dinner he remarked rather pointedly:

Doyle, Ian Hallam and Willi Moore, distinguished team pursuiters all, meet in a 'devil' at the Leicester track

There are youngsters in this club who seem to think that getting to the top is simple. It is not. It is sheer hard work. There are youngsters who have ambitions to get into the 1980 Olympics. To get there you need 100 per cent dedication. You have to live on your bike, and there is not one single member at the moment who is that dedicated.

The following summer, after making his first appearance at the Easter track meeting at Portsmouth, Doyle began riding every Monday and Wednesday evening in the Herne Hill competitions. In fact it became so much part of his routine that he used to leave his track bike in the cabins there, and ride over to the meetings on his road bike. At that time he would ride anything that was going – handicap sprints, regular sprints, devils and long-distance races.

The track sport was very healthy at that time, and a tremendous lot of riders and spectators turned up. Even in the weekly meetings we'd get 150 competitors. On Wednesdays they'd come down from the Midlands, and since that meeting was open to the pros, you'd even get people like Tony Gowland [winner of the Skol 6 at Wembley three years before] turning up.

On Tuesday evenings and at the weekends Doyle would still ride time trials with his old enthusiasm, adding to his titles the Welsh junior 25 and the West London AC junior championship; he had now beaten the hour over 25 miles 11 times. He also renewed his lease on the Bennett Memorial cup. But, actively encouraged by Whiteway, he was becoming increasingly drawn to track racing, and the attraction became even stronger after his first participation that August in the junior track championships at Saffron Lane, Leicester.

This confirmed that he was more than just a local phenomenon. Entering the 3,000 metres pursuit, he was matched for the first time against all the most promising young riders in Britain, and in what had become the most fashionable event for aspiring trackmen and roadmen alike. In the qualifying round he drove round the nine laps in a national junior record time of 3 min 55sec. And although he seemed to misjudge his finishing effort in the semi-finals, in the final for third and fourth he took the bronze by beating Graham Jones, who was to take another path from Doyle's with a long career in continental road racing. It was not a big win. It measured 0.02 of a second, to be pedantic about it. But it provided Doyle with an entrée into the national junior squad, and that winter he joined them in their get-together at Lilleshall in Shropshire.

Doyle now began a new job as a trainee produce buyer with Keymarkets, a supermarket chain of 110 stores. He worked from Sunbury Cross, and what he bought was fruit and veg to be delivered to the firm's three depots. He'd visit Spitalfields and Covent Garden markets and various farms. No two days were alike, each season's produce was different, and he really enjoyed the variety of the work. But although he rose to assistant buyer before he was made redundant in May 1978, during one of those periodic price wars that hit the supermarkets, it was never likely to be a career for life. Doyle was already set on making his way on a bicycle.

All the same, he did not come from a privileged background and had to find a way of subsidising his cycling apprenticeship. Having been helped out by the Clarence with equipment in his early days, as he began to make his name Doyle found a new ally in Geoffrey Butler Cycles of South Croydon who, while never formally his sponsors, kept him in bikes and equipment. And for the rest he scraped by with any prize money he won in competition; this just about covered his fares and, later, his petrol. But there was no cash to be won out of season, so during the winter months of 1978-9 and 1979–80 he took a job in the sports department of Selfridges, London's Oxford Street store, which liked to have leading sportsmen selling its goods; one such was Graham Roope, the Surrey and England cricketer. To get to and from work Doyle cycled the 18 miles, with a little close-formation riding thrown in at Hyde Park Corner

It was at Lilleshall that Doyle first became aware of the junior world championships coming up in Liège the following summer and – in order to improve his performance on the track – of his own need to branch out into road racing.

At that time we were a time-trialling club, so a lot of the hierarchy thought that massed-start racing wasn't quite acceptable. It was the sort of feeling you get in rugby, where the union game doesn't really approve of the league. But I was sure that road racing – riding in formation, reacting to sudden challenges, attacking and chasing – was going to be more beneficial than just sticking to time trials. So from the start of the 1976 season I began to enter road races, though I had to do it on the quiet.

That couldn't have been easy, since in early May he scored a well-publicised victory in the Peak Forest race for under-19s, the second event in the Peter Buckley Trophy series, and only the third road race he had ever ridden. On a wet, overcast day he proved himself a better climber than his lanky figure would suggest, and, in the minds of the northern riders, a more dogged fighter than the south was entitled to produce. On the second climb of Mam Tor near Buxton, and 25 miles from the finish, Doyle went clear alone, and the favourites, who could only do so much chasing, countered half-heartedly, thinking that the head-wind would do the job for them. Far from it. Doyle increased the gap and crossed the line with more than a minute to spare.

So began a season-long campaign in which he was to be the rival of another Home Counties rider, Glen Mitchell of the 34th Nomads, in the Buckley races, and his partner on the track. Doyle won one other race in the series, the Charles Viner Memorial from Coventry to Nottingham – in a split decision by the judges, one of whom gave the sprint to Mitchell while the other three cast their vote for Doyle. Overall it was almost as close up to the final race, the Junior Peaks back in Buxton. With Mitchell already ahead on points, Doyle had to win with his rival unplaced, and he gave it his best throw. But during the race his pedal crank twice worked loose and he was once sent off course. It just wasn't his day.

Still, in most other respects, it was to be his season. Soon after the Peaks Forest race he was told that he had been picked for Liège. And even if the team came back empty-handed – something to which the sport had become inured – they did not return despondent. In place of gold medals there were at least a few silver linings. Enough, anyway, for one of Doyle's local papers, which avidly followed his career from the start, to headline its story: 'Doyle is fifth in the world!' That was his position in the qualifying round of the individual pursuit, though he went out in his next ride to the eventual fourth finisher, Jurgen Lippold of East Germany. In the team pursuit the British juniors – Doyle, Mitchell, Ian Leckenby and Richard Smith – came even closer. They qualified well, but mid-way through the quarter-finals dropped Smith, who was still suffering the effects of an earlier crash when his rear tyre rolled off on the banking. Doyle rode full laps, trying to compensate for Smith's absence, but it was Italy who went through to the semis. 'If we hadn't had that misfortune,' says Doyle, 'I think we could well have gone on to a silver or bronze.' Harry Walker, the Welshman who was track team masseur, agreed: 'We had the legs to beat the Italians. All we needed was average luck.' He also said that in Doyle Britain had 'one of the greatest prospects for a long time'.

Although he was classed a junior by the UCI because he had been 17 at the start of the racing year, under British rules Doyle became a senior just as soon as he passed his eighteenth birthday on 19 May 1976. So it was as a senior that he returned to contest the 4,000 metres individual pursuit and the kilometre time trial at the national championships in Leicester. It was not his debut as a senior. Three or four months after his birthday he had been a last-minute choice by Great Britain for a track international against the Netherlands at Middlesbrough, making up a pursuit team with Steve Heffernan, Ian Hallam and Robin Croker which almost caught, and decisively beat, the Dutch squad.

At Saffron Lane, though, the age-gap was a little too wide to cross at the first attempt. In the pursuit Doyle reached the semi-finals, but there met Heffernan, the current champion, who had been picked only as a reserve for the Olympic team in Montreal and was not in a mood to do anyone favours. He beat Doyle by four seconds before going on to retain his title against Ian Banbury. Meanwhile in the ride-off for the bronze, Doyle lost by two seconds to another of his team-mates at Middlesbrough, the 27-year-old Hallam, an even more experienced rider who had competed in the previous Games at Munich. In the kilometre he came seventh.

On the strength of these solid mid-summer performances Doyle was picked to represent Britain in an amateur six-day race at the Montreal velodrome in November. His partners in a three-man team were Heffernan and Banbury.

It was tremendous for me to get my first senior overseas international at the Olympic venue. And then to be riding alongside Banbury, who had won a bronze medal at the Montreal Games, and Heffernan, who had been to the Olympics, was the reigning British pursuit champion and a Commonwealth Games gold medallist – that was a tremendous experience. And I went out there and I rode really well. I wasn't like the weak link in the team at all.

It was always a tight race between the British, the Italians and the Americans, who were represented by a team from Detroit, a famous centre of pro six-day racing during the 1930s. On the final night the Brits were one lap ahead of Detroit, who held a 35 points lead and would win if only they could steal back a lap to draw level. During their 11th-hour counter-attack, while Heffernan's men rode tenaciously to hold them off, Doyle crashed. He was unhurt, and after trotting back to the cabin to get his wheels changed, was immediately back on the track with 7,000 Canadians cheering him on. The crisis passed, and Britain protected their winning lead to the finish. For Doyle, there could hardly have been a more satisfying end to his first half-season as a senior.

Tom Pinnington, the British team manager, had taken a risk in selecting Doyle for Montreal. There has always been a tendency for riders to treat selection as an end in itself, and any trip abroad as a reward for past success, not as an opportunity to do even better. Doyle was too ambitious to take that attitude. He had certainly worked his passage to Montreal, and so the following April Pinnington decided to send him, with the invariably reliable Hallam, to compete in the Southern Games at Pointe-à-Pierre, Trinidad. A week or so of training and competing in the sun would give him a flying start to a season in which it seemed pretty certain that he would also be representing Britain at the world championships in Venezuela. The winner of the Games was a Dane, Bjarne Sörensen, four years Doyle's senior, who won 4 of the 15 international events spread over five days' competition. Doyle was second overall, with three wins, lapping the field to win the 8,000 metres, and also taking the 10,000 metres and 3,000 metres.

It was now back to earth and up to the heavy wind and rain of the north-west for his first senior road race, the two-day Manchester–Rhyl and back. It was the big early-season event of the time. Forerunner of the Sealink International, and ranking second only to the Milk Race, it attracted most of the current big hitters in that side of the sport: Hallam, Sandy Gilchrist, Dudley Hayton, Paul Carbutt, Des Fretwell, Joe Waugh. As a soft, southern trackie, Doyle was not expected to feature strongly; nor was he over-optimistic himself. But that had been the case the year before in the Peak Forest race, and this time he had the benefit of his warm-up in Trinidad. Placed second on the outward stage, and third on the return, he also collected enough sprint bonuses to beat Waugh by eight seconds. His winner's prize is worth a historical footnote, too: a frameset, half a gallon of vodka and £30.

Doyle continued to ride road races and time trials, though mainly as a build-up for his track programme, and remained a member of the senior Great Britain track squad, attending what, to his mind, were its all too infrequent training sessions. This was a hindrance to the pursuit team, though perhaps no great loss to Doyle himself. In August he returned to Leicester for the national championships and found the opposition in the individual pursuit much depleted. Heffernan had turned professional, Hallam was indisposed and Banbury, having only recently recovered from breaking his leg, was short of preparation. It was virtually a one-horse race, though maybe, with Venezuela in mind, it would have been better for Doyle if there had been a stronger field to take on. He set easily the best time in the qualifying round, and without having to extend himself unduly, beat Banbury in the semi-finals and a former junior champion, Derek Hunt, in the final.

If anything, his second gold medal, shared with Glen Mitchell in the 80km madison, cost him greater effort. They set the pace from the start, and after a three-point penalty for a brush with an opponent who passed on the wrong side, Doyle made certain of victory by taking the double bonus at the final sprint. After that Doyle's selection for the world championships was a matter of course.

Almost everything having gone right for Doyle that season, the events on the San Cristobal track in Venezuela were a bit of a let-down. His best result was in the 50km points race, not simply because he finished fifth, but because he and his team-mate, Hallam, who was fourth, aggressively took the contest to their opponents and led for most of the race, lapping most of

Putting in the last miles of summer with the roadmen. On the Galway–Limerick stage of the 1986 Nissan Classic, Doyle leads the Canadian, Steve Bauer, with Robert Millar and Teun Van Vliet on his right

*Within a few days of retrieving his world pusuit title at Colorado Springs in 1986,
Doyle is back home contesting the Kellogg's city centre race in Westminster . . . and
doing justice to his new rainbow jersey by winning in style*

Doyle took two medals in the 1987 world championships at Vienna – bronze in the pursuit and silver in the 50km points race, which was thrillingly decided only in the final sprint. The points title went to the Swiss Urs Freuler, the bronze medal to Roger Ilegems of Belgium

The old firm of Clark and Doyle have won more often together than any other current partnership on the winter tracks, they have sadly been prevented by the promoters from extending that record to its natural limits

the 34-man field and leading the scoreboard on points. These they picked up for as long as they were in the first four at every fifth crossing of the finish line. But after 70 of the 120 laps an attack by four of the survivors got the better of them. Three of these escapers finished a lap ahead to share the medals among themselves, the gold going to the Belgian, Constant Tourné, now one of Doyle's closest colleagues on the six-day circuit. Despite their long effort and superior tally of points, Hallam and Doyle just missed out.

In the individual pursuit Doyle failed to qualify; in the team event the British got through in seventh place but were knocked out in the quarter-finals. Initially the team consisted of Hallam, Doyle, Mitchell and Paul Fennell, but when Fennell lost contact in the qualifier, Hunt was substituted for the next round. It made little difference. In their quarter-final they were up against the West Germans, winners for the past three years, who had been upset to find that the Germans from east of the 'iron curtain' had set the fastest qualifying time (in fact, the East Germans would go on to beat them in the final). Midway through the pursuit the British team lost Mitchell, who had broken a spoke, and all the efforts of Hallam and Doyle could not prevent the embarrassment of being caught by the Germans.

In retrospect it does not seem too bad a result. The British team reached the last eight in the 1980 Olympics, but since 1977 it has regularly failed to do so (at least up to and including 1991) at a world championships. But at the time it was a disappointment, for the sport had recently become accustomed to being up there with the world leaders in the team pursuit.

The good years had begun at the Munich Olympics of 1972 when a pursuit team made up by Hallam, Mick Bennett, Willi Moore and Ron Keeble beat Poland to take the bronze medal. They were an intelligent and highly motivated group, all pretty experienced in top level competition; Hallam had won a silver medal in the world individual pursuit at Leicester in 1970. Now, having discovered how close they they had come to the top, they were prepared to stay together and work even harder to try and close that gap – and not simply by physical training but by analysing their strengths and weaknesses and refining their technique.

The following year the world championships were held at San Sebastian on a fast, well-seasoned wooden track in an almost enclosed velodrome sheltered from the damp Atlantic weather. There the performance of the team was to peak. They were now without Keeble, but had recruited the young Rik Evans, who could be relied on in the early stages, leaving the other three to go in for the kill. And so it worked out. They reached the final against West Germany, won the gold – and then surrendered it to their

Far from the traffic jams of the six-day track, Doyle crosses the winning line in splendid isolation at Northampton in 1988

opponents in a slightly bizarre display of sportsmanship.

These were the circumstances. The Germans were roughly three seconds up 50 metres before they would reach their station for the final time. But at that point their leading man hit an official who was adjusting the rubber pads on the inside of the track. All four Germans came down with an explosion of bursting tyres. Lutz had a broken collar-bone, Schumacher injured his jaw, and neither of the other two could finish. The British meanwhile crossed the line, and were announced as winners through a pandemonium of whistling. They were embarrassed, knowing that they would have lost but for the accident, and their officials made no counter-claim when the Germans protested. So a team which hadn't completed the race were awarded the gold, 'considering the conditions in which the accident was produced'. And the only team to finish were awarded the silver, though the official result included the comment: 'Great Britain had favourably welcomed the decision in a very sporting way.'

The same team got their gold in 1974, but in the less challenging competition of the Commonwealth Games at Christchurch, New Zealand. And after two blank years in the world championships, it won a further bronze medal by beating East Germany in the 1976 Olympics in Montreal. Hallam and Bennett alone remained of the original hard core, Ian Banbury and Robin Croker making up the team. By the time Doyle joined it at San Cristobal the following summer, only Hallam was left, and he was competing for the last time.

> I came in at the end of an era, which was unfortunate. It meant there was a very strong tradition in team pursuiting. But it wasn't like the individual, where we'd always had a good track record going back to Norman Sheil, Hugh Porter, Tom Simpson. This was more exceptional. The nucleus of that team had spent a lot of time together. They'd ridden stage races together, the Tour of Holland, the Milk Race. And to get anywhere you've got to have the harmony, the spirit of a team, so that you don't just race together, you train and practically live together.

Doyle admired that attitude, but gradually came to realise that recent history was not about to repeat itself.

> We were the beginnings of what might have been another era, but it didn't happen. I mean, we started off as a new team in '77 by qualifying for the world's, so we showed there was some strength in depth. But different riders for different reasons didn't want to commit themselves totally to the track. Derek Hunt, for instance, went on to spend a great deal of time in Holland racing on the road, and he became a professional there and in Belgium. That's where he wanted to make his mark.
> I suppose we were that much younger in the national squad at that

Doyle makes a dramatic start as a senior by winning his first stage race, the 1977 Manchester-Rhyl-Manchester which attracted all the leading amateurs of his day. Here he comes in second at Rhyl ahead of Jim Parry and Steve Jones. He will clinch the victory with sprint bonuses and third place on the return leg

time. We were only just seniors. Everything was ahead of us. So it was difficult to get four riders of equal calibre to show the same commitment as more experienced men who knew exactly what they wanted to get out of the sport.

Doyle, even at 19, was one of the few who did know what he wanted and, seeing his future as a trackman, was willing to make that commitment: 'I'd seen the beginings of what could have been a world-class team and gone on to win the Commonwealth Games at Edmonton at 1978 and do something in the world championships.' But he found little response to his enthusiasm over the next couple of years. Although he continued to ride with the pursuit team in 1978 and 1979, his confidence in it did not perk up again until the run-up to the Moscow Olympics in 1980.

On balance the rewards of 1978 just about outweighed the pain of achieving them. Early in the season he rode the Milan amateur six-day with his old madison partner, Glen Mitchell, and came third on the points table, winning more car tyres, ski boots, training shoes and bottles of wine and liqueur than he could fit into his luggage. And while 20 of the teams were involved in crashes, theirs was one of only two which escaped unscathed. A return to the Montreal 6 – again alongside Mitchell, and with the sprinter, Trevor Gadd, making up the trio – went less smoothly. Doyle had just been made redundant by Keymarkets, and a change of environment did not improve his luck. They were the only team without a manager, and so had no-one to represent them in any dispute with the organisers – a real problem since one unexplained three-point penalty left them in third place overall, one point behind the US team. And although Doyle adroitly steered his way out of one spot of trouble when his tyre blew out on the top of the banking, he crashed badly when he was knocked off by another rider. That night he also developed a fever and stomach trouble.

On the road he won the three-day Ras de Cymru, came third in the Pernod Grand Prix and had his regular clutch of lesser victories. But all this was secondary to his efforts on the track where, on a squad trip to Norway for training and competition, he won the individual pursuit and the points race from his team-mates, and was selected for the Commonwealth Games to be held in Edmonton, Canada, even before his return to Leicester for a successful defence of his national pursuit title.

Edmonton brought him two bronze medals, in the team and the individual pursuit (where he broke Hugh Porter's 12-year-old British record for the Games with a time of 4-53.86), and very nearly a third; he was just edged into fourth place in the 10-mile race. It also brought him a good deal of pain, for in the ride-off against Canada in the team pursuit he badly bruised his back in a kind of accident unlikely to be repeated. His foot slipped from the toe-clip at the start and, expecting a restart he rode to the top of the banking and waited. But no recall gun was fired, and as the Canadians came round he was knocked from his bike.

Altogether, while it may have had its compensations, it had been a pretty frustrating year. Doyle was ready to make a fresh start, which was why, just before Christmas, he was to be seen among the sand dunes at Koksidje in Belgium, riding his first cyclo-cross event. He was not about to take up the sport, but his presence there was his way of reaching a new stage in his career.

A winters tale 7

After more flight problems on the way back from Russia, Doyle arrived home at six in the evening. Twelve hours later he was in the air again, this time with Anne, flying from Gatwick to Orlando. London had turned out to be as cold as Moscow; Florida was in the seventies. It had other attractions for him, too: visiting the Magic Kingdom at Disneyworld, going to the pictures, rising late, and having nothing to do on schedule except two-and-a-half hours light training in the warm outdoors.

He was out training, too, on Christmas morning, and although the holiday had the traditional ingredients of presents, food and family visits – plus their regular dinner guest, Alf Whiteway, by 5.30 am on Boxing Day, Doyle was back on the road. With his brother-in-law Mark for company he drove to Dover, and on from Calais to Dortmund. There he represented the Rest of Europe in a team omnium against Germany, riding alongside Gianni Bugno, the world road race champion, who was making his debut on an indoor track. The match was drawn, and Doyle, having played his part by winning the sprints, was back in the car to reach home by three o'clock the following morning. So began the second half of the season, which continued in earnest four days later.

The one nagging worry at this time was that *The European* had laid off its staff on the day that Doyle flew to Florida. Even though the management decided to keep production going with a skeleton crew, so improving its chances of finding a buyer, there was still a question against its future.

COLOGNE 6

Monday, 30 December

The first day of the Cologne 6 completed, and a load of riders were in trouble because they had let their form slide – either by not training enough since Zurich or Moscow or by indulging too much over Christmas. Also the size of the track came as a big shock – only 166m compared with 333.3m in Moscow and 250m in Zurich.

I am riding with Dean Woods for the first time. Every six-day so far this winter, a new partner. I am becoming a real taxi-driver. There is a new race director here this winter, Wilfred Peffgen, who has taken over after the sudden death in September of Peter Kantas, who was only 45. Peff is very good and experienced, though – a top six-day rider in the past and a former director of the Stuttgart 6.

Tuesday, 31 December

It's very different seeing the New Year in 'on the boards'. The good thing is that the racing finishes early, though up until then it is always fast and furious – and dangerous – as everyone seems out to make an impression. Then at 11.30 pm we all rush to the cabins to get showered and changed into civvies (a rare treat in the middle of a Six), and then dash back to the centre of the track to wait for midnight to strike.

Trestle tables are arranged at the trackside for the riders, wives, girl-friends and family, and drinks and refreshments laid out. All the crowd stay, 8,000 of them, making it one of the biggest parties in Europe. They are treated to indoor fireworks, bands, singers, rock groups. All the earlier arguing and ill-feeling is forgotten. And at midnight we all charge round the track to offer a hand of friendship (!) and to wish the rest a Happy New Year.

The Germans really know how to enjoy themselves, and are putting away the beer and *Sekt* like nobody's business.

Wednesday, 1 January 1992

A lot of the riders' New Year resolutions must have been to try much harder and 'go for it'. The racing today was very fast, and also dangerous with a number of crashes. With the track so small, if anything happens there is no place to go. I was fortunate not to get involved.

What also seems strange is that we still have a couple of days' racing to go. We used to start in Cologne on 27 December, which meant that New Year's Day was the finale. But at least I am having a better Six than last year, when I was riding with Remig Stumpf and we crashed on New Year's Eve. Stumpf dislocated his shoulder, which meant that I was alone at the finish.

The sleeping quarters here are very basic, and at least half the peloton sleeps in hotels. I am at a hotel owned by the parents of the former pro, Josef Kristen, a German who stopped riding a couple of years ago after winning the European madison championship and half a dozen Sixes.

Today you could see several of the riders starting 1992 in the colours of their new sponsors for the season.

Thursday, 2 January

There have been more crashes here than all the winter. Rollerball on wheels! So far I have been okay. The crashes are mainly caused by fatigue and inexperience, and I am pleased that I am going really well. It looks like a couple of riders will have to retire because of their injuries, and new teams will have to be formed.

Andy Kappes and De Wilde are looking very comfortable, having won here for the past two years and at Munich this winter.

Friday, 3 January

What a great atmosphere. Another full house of 8,000 and the public very appreciative of some entertaining racing. It now looks as though the two strongest teams will definitely be fighting it out for the win: Stumpf and Bruno Holenweger versus Kappes and De Wilde. And in the final tomorrow night we can expect much the same tension, which makes it that much more enjoyable.

The racing must be hard when you consider what is happening to the winners of the last two Sixes. Khrabzov and Ganeev, who won in Moscow, are in sixth place at 9 laps. And Joho and Stutz, the Zurich pair, are in seventh place at 11 laps!

Saturday, 4 January

The racing is made much tougher here by the 2–4.30 afternoon sessions, but there was a great last night to this 40th anniversary of the Cologne 6. The final chase was very exciting to watch and take part in. The crowd really got into it. And although we finished fifth, I am very pleased with my form and looking forward to Bremen, where I'm due to be riding once more with Danny. Meanwhile it's nice to go home for a few days, and particularly tomorrow when we are having a family get-together cum New Year celebration.

Result: 1 Remig Stumpf (Ger)/Bruno Holenweger (Swi), 226pts; 2 Kappes (Ger)/De Wilde (Bel), 203pts; 3 Georgen (Ger)/Veggerby (Den), 157pts; 5 Doyle (GB)/Woods (Australia), 83pts, at 3 laps

Chapter 8

Moscow: return to victory

There is nothing sloppy about Doyle. He is a Filofax man; he remembers to do what he says he'll do. And although his style is to appear patient and relaxed – or the term he likes to use, philosophical – things must be just so: his preparation and equipment, his clothes, his home. He is prepared to spend a lot of time and energy and, now that he has it, money, on getting things right. This goes some way to explain why he found the poor performances of the British pursuit team in the 1978 and 1979 world championships particularly galling. It wasn't that the other members of the team lacked ability, though admittedly they were fairly inexperienced; they just didn't seem to him to share his ambition to create a team as disciplined and successful as the one they had succeeded.

There was little that one man could do about it, and he soon recognised that the team pursuit wasn't going to give him an achievable target for the next few years. Instead he decided to concentrate on developing his own abilities as a racing cyclist. Where better to do it than France? And when better to do it than now? There must be many hundreds of talented British riders who have promised themselves a trial season in France, and then dithered until it was too late. Doyle made his move at the beginning of March 1979, a couple of months before his 21st birthday. It was, incidentally, the same year that the Scottish climbing specialist, Robert Millar, joined the influential ACBB club near Paris as the first step towards a prolific career in road racing, and many at home believed that Doyle was taking only a slightly different route to the same destination.

The way Doyle put it to his local paper, the *Staines & Egham News*, was: 'With the poor set-up in Britain – there are no national coaches and very little help for riders – I had no choice but to go abroad. I had intended to go last season but decided to stay and ride in the Commonwealth Games.' And to another journalist Doyle, always a man with specific aims, confided:

Taking French leave from domestic racing in 1979, Doyle is the newest recruit to UC Amnéville/Messina/Maison Phénix. He poses (second from left) with fellow riders after a team launch at the Messina cycle factory. Centre of back row is his team director, Raymond Reisser, a former Tour de France rider

'If I am ever going to break into the professional ranks, this is an opportunity I cannot turn down ... The two things I most need at the moment are a car and a grounding in French.'

He settled in a small town called Woippy, just outside Metz, in the north-east corner of France close to the borders of Belgium – where he regularly competed – Luxemburg and Germany. At the time Metz had a strong connection with British and Irish cycling. This dated back to the earlier 1970s when two well-known British amateurs, Bill Nickson and Jack Kershaw, based themselves there, and was strengthened when Sean Kelly, denied a ride in the 1976 Olympics because he had ridden in South Africa, had instead come to Metz as an amateur, and with a string of successes had attracted the attention of the pro team managers. Metz had two rival amateur clubs, backed by two rival, but highly commercial, building companies. One was VC Metz (sponsor, Maisons Ast), which had been Kelly's club; the other was UC Amnéville (co-sponsors, Maison Phénix and a local cycling factory called Messina), which Doyle joined.

He had laid his plans carefully, with no little help from Johnny Morris, an ebullient cyclo-cross enthusiast who was forever taking parties across to the Continent to race in earnest or for fun, and usually both. In the autumn of 1978, at a big cyclo-cross meeting at Eastway, the custom-built cycle racing circuit in London, Morris introduced Doyle to Raymond Reisser, a former Tour de France rider and Amnéville's *directeur-sportif*, who had brought a team across. The contact made, wheels began to turn. Then in December, Doyle, who hadn't ridden a cyclo-cross since he was a schoolboy, agreed to join Morris and a high-powered team, which included two national cyclo-cross champions, John Atkins and Keith Mernickle, on a weekend racing trip to Belgium and Luxemburg. Conveniently it passed close enough to Metz to allow Morris and Doyle to have dinner with Reisser and his family, and over the meal the offer of a place at Amnéville was made and accepted. Doyle never had any reason to regret it, and neither did the club.

In comparison with the less serious, more social English club scene he had known and thoroughly enjoyed for some years, Doyle now found himself being looked after like a professional. First he stayed with the family of a French rider, and then – a far cry from England, this – was provided with a flat of his own. 'I liked the people I was involved with,' he says. 'I liked the club. Liked the racing and the life-style, and I fitted in very well.' And he liked the life even better when Anne came out to join him in July. 'Living on your own in this flat that the club provided, and not speaking the language, you could feel cut off. But though it's a big step, I'm glad I made it.'

Obviously, too, it helped that he did well on the bike. He won his opening event and by the end of the season had 12 road race victories and 45 first-six places to his credit. He also rode successfully in several high-class stage races, coming second in the Circuit des Ardennes and third in the Circuit des Mines. He was third again in the Grand Prix de France, a 43km time trial in which Graham Jones, Sean Yates, Phil Anderson and Millar, all members of the English-speaking 'new wave', figured in the first ten. The winner was a Danish rider, Hans-Henrik Oersted, who was to remain a thorn in Doyle's flesh for the next decade, though more often in track events than on the road.

His debut race was the 130km Prix Pinchi at Bouligny, where, with his hair plastered down by the rain, he won with what the local paper described as 'an explosive sprint'. It went on:

> One knew that Doyle was fast and above all an excellent pursuiter, and there was the result. At the same time one saw him take the two climbs on the course in his stride, without any apparent discomfort. And meanwhile, if he had held himself back until then it was, so his new team manager, Raymond Reisser, told us, because he was suffering those minor intestinal disorders which affect all foreign roadmen when they first taste rich French cooking.

The French are unshakeable in their belief that the British in particular live on overcooked vegetables and unflavoured meat. Reisser, however, was highly impressed: he had been astonished, he told another reporter, by Doyle's reading of the race and his composure under fire, and he had conducted the sprint like a veteran campaigner.

It was the first of many wins and flattering headlines: 'New Victory for Antony [as they rechristened him] Doyle'; 'Demonstration from Doyle and his Team at Longwy' (he was now its acknowledged leader); 'Crushing Domination of Antony Doyle' (this was in the GP *La Nouvelle Voix de l'Est*, where he won both stages, one of them by over three minutes); 'Doyle Sovereign at Thionville'. Because of his local connections, newspapers in Lorraine even found the space to mention that when he returned briefly to Leicester for the national championships he came away with three gold medals: in the 4km pursuit, the points race and, with Glen Mitchell as his partner, the madison.

All the same, not every one understood this preoccupation with the track, and Doyle himself couldn't quite resolve the dilemma. There was another problem of adjustment when he switched from the fixed wheel of the Leicester track to another six-week spell with variable gears over the bumpy roads of France. It was not the ideal preparation for the world championships in Amsterdam, and Doyle did himself less than justice there. But why bother, thought the French, when Doyle was showing such promise in the far more profitable field of road racing.

True, there were also two disqualifications in France for irregularities in the sprint finishes which gave opponents a closer acquaintance with the barriers than they wanted. These provoked some finger-wagging, but were not held against him for long; in the sprint most disputes are settled on a knock-for-knock basis.

At the end of October Doyle went home for the winter, returning to France just to ride the amateur six-day of Grenoble with a friend from the rival VC Metz, Jean-Pierre Harment, the youngest rider in the field. At the end of the third night they were in the yellow jersey and received a tremendous reception from the crowd. But just to emphasise again the fragility of success in that sport, at the start of the fourth evening Harment fell heavily after colliding with another rider and broke his thigh bone. With no substitute partner on offer, Doyle was forced to drop out of the race.

It was a disappointing end to what had otherwise been a thoroughly encouraging season. Had it given him a taste for road racing? He does not reply directly. 'Well, it gave me a taste of being based on the Continent and so more in touch with the world of cycling, which I already meant to make my career. It broadened my outlook. And yes, it was my intention at that time to look for a road contract.' If he had been ready to sign up then he would not have had far to look. Before the end of the season he had

Nottingham 1983, and a city centre podium for a change. Diagonally from left to right: Doyle, the winner of the criterium; runner-up, the Australian, Steele Bishop; third, Phil Bayton. In front is Phil Thomas, overall leader of the Kellogg's series

In pole position at the start of Kellogg's city centre race and chatting to the Australian, Shane Sutton. On these small, tight circuits it's always better and safer to start, and if possible stay, at the front

Doyle begins to raise his left arm as he crosses the line to win the final stage of the 1985 Sealink International. The rider with both arms aloft is Joey McLoughlin who knows that he has made certain of the overall victory

been approached by Jean-Pierre Danguillaume, *directeur-sportif* of the Miko-Mercier team – and theirs was not the only offer available. Reisser had wide contacts in the sport, and the Messina company, his sponsors, were related through the controlling Deschamps family to two other cycle manufacturers, one of them the well-known La France. 'There were various strings they could have pulled. But I wanted to give the Olympics a go in 1980 and decided to wait. And then everything was altered by what happened at Moscow and afterwards.'

The following February Tony married Anne, took part in a Clarence Wheelers sponsored ride next day (not that club members would have found anything odd in that), and in March he left, with his wife, for Metz once more. But only for two months this time. Then it was back to ride the Sealink stage race, take part in the Olympic trials in May and train for Moscow. Again the French wondered why, if he was so keen on an Olympic medal, he didn't put himself forward for the road race. But it was clear to Doyle that an event with 150 starters, many of them inexperienced in handling their bikes, would be little better than a lottery.

He explained to J B Wadley, the most influential cycling journalist of the post-war years, who was then writing for the *Daily Telegraph*: 'I appreciate that I can serve Britain better on the track. If selected I will put in two months' intense preparation with the squad. Then if we reach the right standard and take the form to Russia, we have an outside chance of a medal.' Wadley, a great francophile, whose first love was outdoor racing, from the tours and classics down to the village *kermesses* of Europe's western seaboard, was not wholly convinced: 'Even an Olympic bronze medal would delight the British cycling world and give Doyle, very much an amateur at heart, immense satisfaction. But it would be little help in getting a professional contract.' Mind, he did allow that if Doyle made a big enough name for himself he could exploit his track-racing prowess in the Sixes.

Although Doyle was anxious to ride the individual pursuit in Moscow, he had not given up on the team pursuit. And this time he sensed that the team – in which he would be riding alongside Malcolm Elliot, Glen Mitchell and Sean Yates, all of whom went on to do well in the sport – was much stronger, more committed and more talented than the year before. Believing that, for all his earlier misgivings, they were now capable of winning a medal, Doyle, as promised, threw himself into the training.

It was one of the most uneasy Olympic meetings in the history of that increasingly contentious event. To protest against the USSR's involvement in Afghanistan, the British prime minister, Margaret Thatcher, asked British athletes to back the US government's plea for a boycott of the Games. Some teams, notably the equestrian competitors, agreed. Others, arguing that an eight-year gap would deny many sportspeople the chance of ever getting to the Olympics, held their ground. But their approach was low-key.

After an unsettling period when there was doubt over whether or not they would be going, the cycling team flew to Moscow on 15 July, just a week before the start of the cycling events. At least they had no complaints with the newly built indoor track at Krylatskoye, out in the Moscow suburbs. The wooden bowl was of Siberian larch, beautifully shaped and remarkably fast, even if the steep end bankings looked a bit daunting to the sprinters. Records were to tumble in almost every event. So far, so good. But among the loose ends left during the on-off preparations was who should represent Britain in the 4km individual pursuit.

Only one rider was permitted to do so, and since he would have to come from a pursuit team, this effectively narrowed the choice down to Doyle, the national champion, and Sean Yates, who had taken the silver medal at Leicester in 1979 and given him the only serious competition. Doyle's junior by exactly two years and a day, Yates had a startling turn of speed and was certainly an exciting prospect, but although he had been now riding the road in France he lacked Doyle's international experience on the track. Doyle believed that on the grounds of proven ability – not to mention loyalty, since he had postponed the start of his professional career to be in Moscow – he might have expected to get the nod.

Instead, apparently to settle a matter which was still in doubt, Willi Moore, the track coach, announced that he would organise a private ride-off at Krylatskoye, with the winner – or so Doyle assumed – to get the nomination. This was to take place early in the morning of the 18th, four days before the qualifying round began. It was a curious decision and had an even more bizarre outcome.

The pursuit was run under match conditions, and Doyle won it decisively, setting a personal best time of 4-42 with Yates retiring two-and-a-half laps before the finish. 'So I thought,' says Doyle, 'that we'd got it all sorted out. Obviously I was in very good form, with a real chance of a medal. We went back to the Olympic Village, and that's when Jim Hendry, who was the overall team manager, called us both into his room and announced that Sean was riding and not me. I was dumbfounded.'

Hendry told the *Daily Telegraph* that the reason Yates dropped out was that he had a nose-bleed and had not been able to hear the lap count: 'I have to rely on my own intuition in cases like this, and I have decided that Yates is a better man. Doyle can be suspect. He has had his chances in the past and, to be frank, he has disappointed.' This was news to Doyle: 'If he had a nose-bleed it certainly wasn't gushing out.' And he couldn't credit that a man who had ridden in championships would lose count of the laps. 'I know I beat him comfortably, and I'm under the impression that he cracked.'

Hendry's version of the event is rather different. He says that Moore had wanted to organise the match, and he had allowed it to go ahead – though

121

he had not attended it himself and 'on reflection I think it was a mistake to allow it, since it could only create bad feeling.' And that was what had happened, dividing the team into pro-Yates and pro-Doyle camps.

In Hendry's mind Yates had always been the man who would ride the individual, and he had based that decision on Yates's pursuit victory a month or so before in the Coupe d'Europe, where he had also returned a 4-42 and Doyle had been placed second. It would have needed a 'tremendous' performance by Doyle to change his mind. Since Yates's 4-42 had been set on an outdoor track, Doyle's matching time indoors did nothing to alter that situation. 'I know it was disappointing for Doyle, coming at the pinnacle of his career, but it was down to someone to decide who was right and wrong. And anyway Doyle was still going to be doing what he went there for, ride the team pursuit.'

Doyle acknowledges that Yates then rode pretty well in the individual pursuit. He qualified in seventh place with a 4-44, and improved that to 4-41 in the quarter-finals, but still lost by three seconds to the eventual bronze medallist, the ineluctable Oersted. The title went to the Swiss, Robert Dill-Bundi, from the Frenchman, Alain Bondue.

It's nothing personal. I get on very well with Sean, I've got the utmost respect for him. He's the most underestimated British bike rider – particularly by the British fraternity. On the Continent he's highly appreciated. Well, just look at his stage wins in the Tour de France, Tour of Spain and the Paris–Nice. Then going on to win the Tour of Belgium and finish second in the Tour of Holland. No, it's the way it was done that I object to. And obviously it was disappointing because I knew that was the only Olympics I would ever ride.

The incident did nothing to settle the minds of the pursuit team, but there were no evident signs of dissension in the qualifying round. Riding unopposed on the track they recorded 4-19.73, beating the official world record by over three seconds. That was remarkable for a British team, even if the first eight qualifiers beat it too and the USSR set a new mark of 4-16.62. It left Great Britain in fifth place with a quarter-final draw against the fourth-fastest team, Czechoslovakia.

There everything fell apart when Yates got dropped after eight and a half laps with still a little over a kilometre to go – demoralised, Hendry believes, by the dissension in the team. With Doyle riding full laps at the front, the

Doyle shoots down the ramp at the start of the time trial stage in the Nissan Classic of 1989, the year that Greg LeMond introduced triathlon bars to the Tour de France. At once they joined disc wheels as essential parts of tester's equipment

remaining three held the Czechs until, with just a lap or so to go, Malcolm Elliott lost the wheel ahead of him. Glen Mitchell and Doyle rode on unaware of this, and coming to the line thought they had won until they realised that Elliott – the essential third man whose time would count for them all – was off the back. They were to lose by five seconds. The months of hard training had been wasted.

Doyle didn't blame Elliott: 'Malcolm was a couple of years younger than us, and although he oozed class, he was that little bit inexperienced.' Nor did he hold it personally against Yates. But he found it hard to forgive Hendry for taking what he was convinced was the wrong option over the individual event. And he found Hendry's attitude insensitive. 'When he told us that Sean would get the ride he said he could understand my disappointment. At one time he had expected to get into the Scottish team for the Commonwealth Games, and in the end he hadn't been selected. Well!' It was not the kind of comparison that Doyle cared to make. He was also incensed by an incident which, he said, followed the team's defeat. 'We'd been riding these white-stripe Clement tyres. Very light, four ounces, you could only use them for two rides. So Glen and me were in tears, really inconsolable, and Hendry came into the cabin and told the mechanic, "The lads won't be needing those tyres, you can take them off." It was like taking the rings off the dead.'

Doyle still believes that Hendry's decision to drop him in favour of Yates not only cost him but cost the team a possible medal. 'It's physically and mentally very draining to ride more than one championship, and to build yourself up and come back from disappointment in the second event if you haven't got a medal from the first. If Sean had only had to concentrate on one event, I don't think he would have let the team down.' But why should Doyle think that, if their roles had been reversed, he could have coped any better?

Because I had been to the world championships before and ridden both the individual and team pursuits. And while I wasn't an old man, I was a little bit more experienced. Had I won the individual I would have towed the team round for 4,000 metres. No, seriously, I was obviously in form and would have been in contention. I can't say I was sure to win, but I feel confident that I could have had a medal. That would only have enhanced the team. It would have enhanced my performance, and I think it would have lifted the morale of the whole team.

Summer on the road may be less arduous than winter on the tracks, but there's always the next world championship to prepare for. This keeps Doyle competing for 11 months of the year. Here he is leading Joey McLoughlin in a criterium at Cambridge in 1985, and three years later at a road race at Northampton

All this, of course, is highly conjectural, and when I suggested that Hendry might have thought his strength was more important to the team, and ought to be conserved, he wouldn't have it. Twelve years on, although he insists that the affair doesn't rankle – 'I've accepted it, it's just water under the bridge' – he still sees it in personal terms, softening his bitterness with facetiousness.

I don't know whether he didn't like the after-shave I was using. Or whether it was the fact that he was Scottish and I was English. There is no reason, there is no logic. I never had any real problems, a real set-to. I'd stand up for myself and speak my mind. But I wasn't really anti-establishment and anti-federation and shouting my mouth off. So whether it was a clash of personalities I don't know. I was unaware of it until the decision was made.

Doyle returned home on 28 July, 'very despondent about what happened in Moscow', said his father, 'and I cannot say I blame him.' But it was not a reaction to those events – although that was the popular reading at the time – which provoked him into visiting the BCF offices in London on 4 August, writing out a cheque for £12.50 and signing a declaration form which turned him into an as-yet unsponsored professional. Before the Olympics he had already accepted the offer of a ride in the Skol 6 at Wembley in late September. And oddly, the only thing that might have prevented him from taking it up was winning a medal in Moscow. Then he would not have been allowed to turn professional until the following January. I wondered whether that would have altered the future pattern of his career, diverting him towards road racing. 'No, I think I would still have wanted to get involved with the six-day and the world of the indoor tracks. That was the lure I was attracted to.'

The only backing he had at the time of turning pro was from Geoffrey Butler Cycles, who informally supplied his bikes and equipment. He still needed a sponsor to help with his other expenses, and had already received some approaches, but it was 14 August before he signed with the KP Crisps-Viscount team. The deal was hatched so quickly that there wasn't time for Viscount Cycles to build his machines for that season, and he continued to rely on Geoffrey Butler as he had for the Olympics. But Viscount provided his bikes for the next two seasons, and so began a long and varied association with trade sponsors like Ernie Clements, Holdsworth, Amoco, Carrera-Halfords, and frame-builders Mike Mullett and Chas Roberts. Yet while Doyle can reel off their names and dates, and those of the accessories (Shimano, Mavic, Campagnolo, Gipiemme and Shimano again) and tyres (Clement, Wolber, Michelin, Continental) he has been contracted to use, Doyle is not really one of those riders who like nothing better than tinkering with oily spare parts in his garage. For him bikes are the means to an end – winning races.

By joining KP Crisps-Viscount Doyle hadn't struck it rich exactly. The contract ran for only two months at £150 a month – less than he had been earning as a sales assistant at Selfridges. But it meant that he would be riding alongside two of the great characters of the time, the highly accomplished pursuiter, Ian Hallam, and the indefatigable Phil Bayton, capable of towing the peloton along for mile after mile and known in the sport as the Staffordshire engine.

Doyle's first professional appearance came the following week in the national track championships at Saffron Lane, Leicester, where he would have to adjust to the greater distance of 5km for the professional pursuit. It only needed the qualifying round to show that the extra 1,000 metres was no problem. Matched against Steve Heffernan, who had won the national title both as amateur and professional, and a bronze medallist in the 1977 world's, Doyle kept the gap to a fraction of a second either way up to the half-distance, and then drew ahead to win by four seconds. After a virtual ride-over in the quarter-finals, when his opponent's foot slipped out of a toe-clip in the first lap, Doyle beat Heffernan once more in the semis, this time by ten seconds, and so faced his KP team-mate, the battle-hardened Hallam, in the final.

Hallam did Doyle no favours, making a fast start to try and unsettle his younger opponent. But Doyle was unshaken, and taking charge from the third of 15 laps, steadily made ground. On the final lap he sprinted and came close to catching Hallam, but instead was happy to settle for a 12 sec win. Except for the omnium on the opening weekend of the championships, in which he came third, Doyle had done no trackwork since his return from Moscow. Now he had the title, and felt he had proved the selectors wrong, but he wasn't yet ready to rest his case.

Two weeks away were the world championships in the French city of Besançon, near the Swiss border. Still highly charged, Doyle was determined to make an equal impact there, training hard and leaving on 30 August to give himself four days to settle in before the competition began. With him were Geoff Cooke, the professionals' national track coach, who was to become a regular member of his backing group at the world's; Hallam, who was also to contest the pursuit and finish eighth; and the mechanic, Steve Snowling.

The qualifying round was held on the evening of 3 September, with 21 riders – ten heats of two, plus one man with only himself to compete against – striving to set times which would take them through to the last eight. Doyle's best time over 5km on the timber track at Saffron Lane had been 6-14, and there was some concern among the Brits when the first two riders clocked 6-11 and 6-12 on what was assumed to be Besancon's slower cement surface.

A time of 6-6.5 followed in the third heat, and the favourites were still to come.

Lining up fourth against Dirk Baert, a fast starter who was pushing a bigger gear, Doyle held the Belgian to less than a second for several laps, and then at the halfway stage eased ahead to beat him. Not that victory in itself mattered, but the time certainly did, and it was 6-5.53. In a fortnight's intense training, Doyle had improved by nine seconds, cement or no. He was the fourth fastest qualifier behind the leader, Oersted, another new pro, who returned the only sub-six-minute ride. Doyle, in fact, was faster than the title holder, Bert Oosterbosch of the Netherlands, the winner at Amsterdam in 1979. And for his troubles Doyle won the privilege of meeting Oosterbosch in the quarter-finals next day. It was enough for Doyle at present that he had got through. 'The fact that I was riding against the reigning world champ obviously made me think, but it didn't frighten me off.'

If the qualifying round had gone smoothly, the quarter-final was full of incident and controversy. Doyle was a quarter of a second down at the end of the first lap; level at the end of the second; and then, roughly halfway round the third, when he had begun to press ahead, he punctured. The rules are that if a rider punctures in the first kilometre, the race is re-run over the full distance. If he does so in the final kilometre, the leader is given the race. But if he punctures in the 2nd–4th kilometre, the race is restarted to the nearest half-lap, with one rider given whatever lead he had gained when the puncture occured.

Judging the precise distance of that lead opens up a situation ripe for litigation by an astute team manager. And Peter Post, record six-day man and now Oosterbosch's TI-Raleigh manager, was one of the most accomplished barrack-room lawyers of his or any other day. There was first an argument over whether the stoppage had occurred in or after the first kilometre (not a straightforward matter since the track measured an odd 545m). Then when it was agreed that it had been in the second kilometre, there was a further dispute over what the gap had been.

Doing his best to ignore it, Doyle had his wheel changed, got on his road bike and slowly rode round the inside of the track to keep his muscles loose.

I think one of the reasons Post was making this fuss was to try and unnerve me. He was a really experienced *directeur-sportif* and knew what he was doing. But it didn't have that effect on me, I was totally relaxed. In fact I

At Besançon in 1980, in the brief interval between turning pro and gaining his first world title, Doyle talks to the most influential of cycling writers, JB 'Jock' Wadley of the Daily Telegraph

think it helped me. The crowd realised that he was playing up, and they got behind me even more. I had already gone down well with them after the announcement that I had been racing in France.

Eventually the 20m or so advantage, which Doyle had first been given, was whittled down to 4m, and the riders restarted to cover the remainder of the distance. First blood to Doyle, 1.75 sec up after a further couple of laps; counter-attack by Oosterbosch, who reduced the gap to 0.40sec; but Doyle kept his nose in front to the finish. This only brought further confusion, however, since Doyle got the bell for the final lap almost simultaneously with Oosterbosch getting the finishing gun. Having kept his own count Doyle finished strongly while Oosterbosch faltered, and despite further objections from Post, the jury found for Doyle. More than that, he was given a calculated time of 6-0.67, the fastest of the night.

The final day brought more literal thunderstorms, heavy rain delaying the start of the semis by over two hours and pushing the final on past midnight. Doyle's semi against the Italian, Luciano Borgognoni, was straightforward. Having countered his opponent's fast start, he won comfortably by over three seconds, easing a little to save himself for the final. There he was to meet another Dutchman, Herman Ponsteen, who had beaten Oersted in the other semi-final, though only by going to the limits. Ponsteen was a strong, burly man, but it was asking a lot to expect him to display that form twice in a day.

He also had the disadvantages, as well as the benefits, of coming to the final with a past: an amateur silver medal in 1973, the bronze as a professional the previous year, and now having put out the favourite. The pressure of public expectation lay on him, while there were only hopes for Doyle; it was already marvellous that he had come so far so soon. It turned out to be one of the great finals, with the differences measured in fractions for the first four kilometres. In fact at one half-lap just after midway the two men crossed the line level to a hundredth of a second; if there was a gap it was too small for the Longines timing to measure. Hallam was at the side of the track calling the other gaps, and as a visual aid Geoff Cooke was standing back or forward from the line to show the difference. The British fans were willing Doyle on and the home spectators, too, without a rider of their own to support, had adopted him as their own both because of his French connections and in sympathetic memory of the troubles he had been through the night before. Also there was the Cooke factor. As Doyle recalls, 'He was fantastic. He's such an enthusiastic character, and was jumping up and down, and the crowd were feeding off him.'

When Doyle began to go ahead in the last two kilometres, he did so progressively, keeping up a steady pedalling stroke while Ponsteen found it increasingly hard to maintain his rhythm with a bigger gear. The gap widened, 0.23sec, 0.46, 0.73, 0.78, finally breaking the one-second barrier, and still Doyle pressed home his advantage. At the bell it was 4.27sec, and in the final lap, such was Ponsteen's collapse, he more than doubled that. Just before one in the morning, and to his great satisfaction, Doyle had made himself world champion.

At the semi-final stage, Hendry acknowledged to Ken Evans, the editor of *Cycling*, that he had made the wrong choice in Moscow. 'I'll admit it, but not yet. I don't want Tony to stop hating until after the final.' Evans, however, decently refusing to exploit the benefit of hindsight, came down on Hendry's side. He thought Hendry had been right, and that he had 'provided the motivation which Doyle had hitherto been lacking. For Doyle, the product of a traditional pursuiting school, riding fixed-wheel time trials with the Clarence Wheelers as a young lad, is a gentle soul. Mere encouragement, even full-throated shouts, is not enough to lift him from his normally talented plane. It needed bare rejection to do that.'

It's not a matter that can be proved either way, even by a world medal. There are no retrospective Olympic titles. But Hendry's view that it was all for the best still leaves Doyle cold. 'I let my legs do the talking,' he declares, even though he has also been known to say a few words on the subject. And in the end it was the most eloquent way of writing an epitaph on the whole episode. Nor did he forget his thank-you letters. Before he left France he travelled back to Amnéville to a celebration in the casino where, under Reisser's benevolent eyes, he presented his newly won rainbow jersey to the mayor. 'It was a gesture which went right to the heart of the elected officials,' the local paper noted. 'And the municipality will not forget,' said the mayor.

Back home Doyle picked up the everyday threads of his new professional life. He rode his first professional road race, a criterium at Newport in Wales, where he took it in turn to attack with his team-mate, Bayton, who went on to win. He knew that if he did reasonably well on the road, he would improve his chance of a contract – on rather better terms – for the following year, and events like this were to become the staple activity of his future summers. But more than ever he saw his future on the track, and within a fortnight he might have been seen driving round the south circular on the way to Wembley, a bed and mattress tied to the roof-rack of his car. He was about to ride his first six-day race, the last Skol 6.

A winter's tale 8

During the next Six, at Bremen, Doyle was relieved to hear that *The European* had found new owners, the Scottish twin brothers, David and Frederick Barclay. Whether or not they would want to extend their business interests into sponsoring six-day riders after Doyle's present contract expired at the end of March, at least he could feel secure for the rest of the winter season.

Doyle was also pleased to be paired once more with Danny Clark, though with his old partner hit by jetlag after returning from a Christmas break in Tasmania, they would form a slightly less dynamic duo than usual, at least in the opening days of the race.

BREMEN 6

Thursday, 9 January

It was nice to return to Bremen after an absence of three years. The last time I rode here was with Didi Thurau in 1989; it was his penultimate Six. Then the next two years I missed the event after accidents. And literally missed it, because there is always a great atmosphere and a large crowd here.

Another rider to return was Urs Freuler. But in his case it was after a six-month ban for being found positive with testosterone at the end of the Coca-Cola series of criteriums in July.

Compared with how it used to be, we are nowadays spoilt with our accommodation. We stay in the 5-star Park Hotel, which is somewhat better than the cabins at the track.

As always a great fuss was made of the opening ceremony, with Bud Spencer as the official starter. Not quite as attractive as Florence Joyner Griffiths, who started the race last time I was here!

Friday, 10 January

Full yet again with 18,000 spectators crammed up to the rafters. The amount of beer consumed is incredible. They put it away in vast quantities and really let themselves go, singing along with the popular Klaus & Klaus, a German version of Chas and Dave who really get the packed crowd joining in.

The atmosphere here is unique, and it's surprising that Beck's, the local brewers, have anything left to export.

What with racing from 2 to 5 in the afternoon, and with an evening session which starts at 8 pm and goes on until 3.15 in the morning, we don't fully appreciate the sing-along.

Adriano Baffi is making this year's début on the boards at Bremen. He won at Zurich last winter and is a very accomplished six-day rider. You can be sure he's not riding here and at Antwerp just for the money, but because it is also ideal preparation for the summer season. He is really determined to make his mark on the roads this year, especially after breaking his collarbone in the Giro last June and having to play second fiddle to his teammates, Argentin and Sörensen.

Saturday, 11 January

Belgian riders were the main topic of conversation here today when it was announced that Etienne De Wilde was facing one week in jail and a £1,000 fine after a judge reversed a decision over a controversial positive dope test at Antwerp five years ago. They never let sleeping dogs lie.

The evening session was marred by incidents during the derny races. In the first I blew a rear tyre before going on to win the race. I ruined a new pair of shorts! Then in the second, Andy Kappes did the same. This caused him to crash, bringing down Stan Tourné, who needed a hospital X-ray for a damaged right elbow. The dernys are going so fast on a 166m track and becoming really dangerous.

Sunday, 12 January

And I thought Sunday was supposed to be a day of rest. We raced until 3.15 am, and then we were back on the track from 11.30 am until 6.0 pm. At least we finished early and could be thankful for small mercies. Early sessions on the track are always perilous. Everyone is tired so that the reflexes and reactions are that much slower. Still, we survived without mishap and it made a pleasant change to have an evening off to relax.

Monday, 13 January

The problem here is that the chases are too short – only two of 40 minutes each evening, which is not long enough for us to assert ourselves. The modern approach, in which there are shorter madisons and every 100 points is converted into a lap bonus, gets away from the original format of the Six where the winners were the best team in the chases.

Tonight the first chase was a handicap, and we certainly had the other top teams worried. And in the second chase we were again the strongest, but 40 minutes is nothing like enough. We are both riding really well now, and we can only wish there was a 75km chase to prove our point.

The Stadthalle continues to be packed, but to race until 3 am on a Monday night is uncalled for. At least the programme here is easier than

133

when I began. Then it was seven days long and every afternoon. We must be getting soft!

Tuesday, 14 January

After finishing third for the third time, we are desperate for a win together this season. Only one more chance when we race as a team in the final Six of the winter. So it's Copenhagen or bust!

At least it was a popular victory with the home-town boy, Kappes, winning with De Wilde for the second year in succession. A really thrilling and hard-fought final. All credit, too, to Freuler for finishing second in his first Six of the winter. Obviously the enforced rest, his keenness, and having a point to prove were the major factors.

The track was in fairly poor condition, breaking up in places and needing constant attention. Obviously, putting it up only 24 hours before the race began was not ideal.

At least we won some decent primes for a change, with a fax machine and a video recorder each.

Unusually, we had a lavish reception at the Park Hotel afterwards. At most Sixes it's pack as quick as possible and then dash off to the next one. But considering that around 130,000 spectators came through the turnstiles, I think we deserved it, don't you?

Wednesday, 15 January

Another hectic day at home. Press interviews, several meetings, calls to mates by the dozen, letters and faxes to sort – plus light training. I know I should have stayed in bed this morning instead of getting up at 6.15 to catch the plane. Still, no place like home.

Result: 1 Andres Kappes (Ger)/Etienne De Wilde (Bel), 479pts; 2 Holenweger/Freuler (Swi), 504pts; 3 Clark (Australia)/Doyle (GB), 373pts

Chapter 9

Hard days at the oval office

It amuses Doyle that while most of the neighbours who share his stockbroker housing estate in Surrey drive off to London each morning in their Rovers and BMWs, he wheels a Halford's road bike out of his double garage and pedals off past their coiffured front gardens. But it's all work. The bike is his desk and, as he frequently says, the indoor tracks of Europe are his office. The job is a bit more strenuous and dangerous than selling insurance in the City, and the hours are certainly more unsocial – eight in the evening to two-thirty the following morning very often, and no free weekends or holidays. But Doyle simply thinks he's lucky to be paid for cycle racing, which is what he'd be doing in his spare time anyway, just for the love of it.

That 19 September, when he drove to Wembley with a bed and mattress on his roof-rack, along with his bikes and wheels, was the true start of it. He might be the new world pursuit champion, but at the Skol 6 he was – to continue his analogy – just the new office boy. And the reason, by the way, that he was carrying his own bedding was that he'd been warned that the overnight accommodation was pretty spartan. The riders would be sleeping in cabins below the track which were normally used by performers for changing or storing their equipment. And unless he brought his own, he'd be sleeping on a basic ex-War Department camp bed. It was a fairly brutal introduction to what he could expect from now on.

His other concern was that he was unfamiliar with the 160m Skol 6 track – except from the spectator's point of view. And since it was specially erected for the event, there was no time to train on it beforehand. He had experience – not all of it happy – of the original Skol 6 track built for Earl's Court in 1967 and later moved to Calshot on the Solent. This had started off only 290ft (105.76m) long, and had been further shortened to fit into what had been a Sunderland flying boat hangar. Doyle had also ridden on other small tracks in Europe as an amateur, but it was not the same thing.

Doyle's gear for a business meeting in London, 1987. Notable features: dark suit, discreet tie, hint of pocket handkerchief, well-buffed shoes, executive briefcase

I wouldn't say I was really nervous, but I was apprehensive. And also because I was about to compete against my heroes. Patrick Sercu, René Pijnen ... until shortly before I'd still had their pictures up on my bedroom wall. They were the guys I'd go and watch at Wembley night after night. I was really enthralled by six-day racing. So one minute you're looking up to your idols, and the next you're lining up alongside them. I suppose in my mind the big dread was to make a mistake and bring Sercu off. But your strongest instinct is to survive, to get around.

Doyle doesn't pretend that he found it easy to adjust:

It was so very different from any form of racing I'd known as an amateur. I mean, I'd ridden amateur Sixes, but they usually consisted of an hour's madison each night, and that was it. The hurly-burly of a pro six was something else again. It's not just on the bikes that the racing is so fast. You've just ridden an hour-long madison, say, putting in one hundred per cent effort, but there's no chance of collapsing in a heap and then going off to rest and have a drink. No, one of the team has to come off the track, be quickly washed and cologned down by his soigneur, put on a new undervest and racing jersey, and get back on his bike so that his partner can come down and change. It's straight on to the next event, which may be a devil, or a series of sprints or a points race or whatever. There's always something happening.

At first I found myself constantly looking at the programme because I was used to riding in open track meetings where you might make three or four appearances in a whole day. Here it was one event after another. And remember, I was riding the Six in my own country, where at least I understood what has happening. I could read the programme and make out what the announcer was saying. So it was better at Wembley than it was going to be abroad. All the same I found it very difficult.

It might have been even more difficult if Ron Webb, organiser of the Skol 6, hadn't found him an experienced and congenial partner. This was the 35-year-old West German, Udo Hempel, who had turned professional after winning team pursuit gold medals at the world's and the Munich Olympics of 1972. Perhaps because he was in his late 20s before he came into the Sixes, he never caught the limelight. But, respected by the promoters as a solid craftsman on the boards, he was much in demand for nursing along what the programme described as 'the local matadors'. In this case, Doyle.

For a newcomer Doyle did well. With Hempel's guidance reinforced by his own determination, they finished a respectable eighth, 20 laps down on the Aussie winners, Danny Clark and Don Allen.

137

They can't go no meeting like this – but they do. This time it's Doyle versus Oersted in an omnium at Herne Hill on Good Friday 1983. They are supported by the brothers Paul, and Keith Wingrave

I was hoping to make a name for myself in the Sixes, and although I was worried I didn't ever think it was going to be beyond me. Lots of riders come in first time, and it's just too much for them, they can't cope. It's not only the physical effort. You have to stay alert. You can't let your mind wander. That's what makes it so different from riding on the road. On a long stage on the road, it's not flat out all the time. There's probably a lull early on or at the feeding station. But in the Sixes, with all the other riders around you on the tight banking, you can't afford to lose your concentration for a moment.

One of the other biggest problems for new riders is that after the evening's racing they go and have something to eat, they wash and change, and then they find they can't wind down. They are still so hyped up, so tense, that they're unable to switch off and go to bed. And that only increases their problems the next day. The reason why there are so many crashes is that tired riders' reactions are obviously slower. That's why you'll notice that they often happen on a Sunday morning. You may have been racing until four that morning and be back on the track by one. And since you have to be up at ten for something to eat, you've had maybe only five hours rest.

It's not always simple to predict who will accommodate to these frenetic conditions and who will find them simply unbearable.

Take Francis Castaing. A very accomplished roadman sprinter who'd won any number of top racing. Well, he'd be mixing it with the likes of Walter Planckaert, Sean Kelly, Jan Raas, risking life and limb, throwing hooks and switches. You'd think he'd be a natural. He came to ride at Dortmund, the third Six that season, and had a good partner, the pursuiter, Alain Bondue. But he rode 10–15 minutes of the first chase, and that was it. He just couldn't handle it. He was totally shell-shocked. Now you would think that someone like him, fearless in the bunch sprints, would be able to adapt.

Or take Kelly himself, a fantastic bike rider, look at his sprinting prowess. Over the years the promoters have been very keen to attract him. But because he doesn't have a background in track cycling he just finds the thought too daunting.

After Wembley came Berlin and Dortmund. They were major events which drew promoters from most of the other Sixes and all the top six-day riders. In a way these two events served as an audition for the rest of the season, one side looking for exciting performers who would bring in the crowds, and the other straining to impress and so win contracts for the rest of the winter. Doyle found that this made the racing extremely demanding: 'At that time we were on each afternoon from two to five, and each evening from eight to two or two-thirty the next morning. Fridays and Saturdays it was 4 pm to 4.30 am – plus you were back on the track on Sunday morning. That's a tradition in Germany; the dads bring along the children, who get in free, and the mums stay home and make the dinner.'

The accommodation in Berlin, too, was so austere as to make Wembley seem luxurious. All the riders were put up at the track, and just when he needed all the rest he could get, Doyle found himself sharing a cabin with six others. It was also next to the showers and lavatories, where the cleaners came and went all night and sleep was constantly interrupted.

Doyle had another established minder at Berlin, a German fifth-year pro, Horst Schutz – a past national sprint and motorpaced champion who had a reputation as a hard man – and together they finished seventh at 18 laps, one up on Wembley. After that, Dortmund, with the one rest-day in between swallowed up by packing, driving and unpacking, though at least it was in a hotel room this time. 'Well, by this time I was just smashed, I didn't know where I was. I just hung on in there, got round and finished. It was a case of being thrown in and either you'd sink or swim. I suppose you could say I managed to paddle.'

Again Doyle found himself with a German partner, this time Gunther Schumacher, another member of that great pursuit team which had won both Olympic titles in the 1970s. He admits that because of his nationality he began to feel an outsider in the Sixes. The only other Briton involved was Maurice Burton, who was also the only black rider on the circuit, and the only other English-speakers were Clark and Allen. This made it harder for him to fit in as a newcomer than it was for the numerous Dutch, Belgians and Germans. He also felt some constraint, as a new pro, in having a rainbow jersey on his back. It had obviously earned him contracts, but initially he thinks that it might also have upset some of the old guard.

Burton, from Catford, was a talented sprinter who had ridden for England in the Commonwealth Games and later settled in Ghent, where he spent the summer racing over the cobbles in the local *kermesses*. He had adapted well to the Continent and to the Sixes, and that winter rode 14 events to Doyle's 9. It was only in the second part of the season that the logical thing was done and they were paired together at Rotterdam and Copenhagen, where they finished sixth and fifth. The latter was Doyle's best result that season when, having started at the top in Besançon, he had gone back to the bottom to work his way up in another branch of the sport. One where nothing is made easy for the beginner, who is treated much like a fag in an old-fashioned public school. 'I was determined to make the grade,' says Doyle. 'It might be difficult, but if others could handle it I knew that, given time, I could do the same. So I persevered and stuck it.'

One encouraging souvenir of that first winter season was a bronze medal from the European omnium championship at Zurich, and it was all the more memorable because it was Patrick Sercu's – Doyle himself had won the silver. The two medals were accidentally switched at the presentation ceremony, and since they didn't notice the mistake until they got home, they never bothered to correct it. The championship, won by the Swiss, Urs Freuler, was made up of a devil, a 10km points race, a flying kilometre and a 4km pursuit, and the best moment came when Sercu approached Doyle just before the pursuit to say, 'Now don't make me look stupid. Just be sure you don't catch me.' Doyle felt immensely flattered: 'To a lad just breaking into the six-days, for the top man to say that was a real compliment.'

Doyle's fixed ambitions on the track strongly influenced his decision to renew his contract with KP for 1981. He had been approached by several big teams on the Continent and took their offers seriously, but he decided that, being still young and relatively inexperienced, he did not want to go immediately from a hard winter's racing to the stress of a European season

Lap of honour in Leicester in 1987 after Doyle had beaten the Italian master, Francesco Moser, in a challenge pursuit match

Greg LeMond, first American to win the Tour de France and now the world's highest paid cyclist, has ridden only one Six – at Grenoble in 1988. Doyle lent nine years' experience to the partnership and they finished fifth

on the roads, where again he would be the new boy with much to learn. He had made a mark in the six-day world, and didn't want to risk sacrificing what he had gained – 'It might all have been too much for me.' And there was another factor. The world championships were taking place in Britain in 1982, and KP, part of the United Biscuits group, were planning to get more and more involved. Having settled for a summer of domestic road races as part of his build-up to the coming world championships in Czechoslovakia and the next round of Sixes, he rode abroad only in some Belgian *kermesses* at the prompting of his co-sponsor, Viscount Cycles.

As it turned out, a training accident at Herne Hill (of which, more in the next chapter) prevented him defending his world title in Brno, and so there was rather less demand for his services in the Sixes. He had also lost his showpiece event, the Skol 6, which had closed after an almost continuous run of 14 years, not from lack of public interest but because the cost of hiring the Wembley Arena made no allowance for those extra days with no gate receipts when the track was being built or dismantled.

With his winter programme reduced to half-a-dozen Sixes, Doyle suffered further setbacks when he crashed at Dortmund in the season's second event – needing hospital treatment for cuts and concussion – and then returned home to find that KP had withdrawn from sponsorship. Again there were offers from the Continent, and one of them, from Peter Post's TI-Raleigh team based in the Netherlands, worth a basic £14,000 a year, was attractive enough for Doyle to follow up. But when talks broke down over terms, he once more opted for a British backer. It was Viscount Cycles, his old co-sponsors, who went on to recruit Ian Hallam and Tony James to form the three-man Viscount-Shimano team. And when Viscount went out of business the following winter, it was RMC (Ready Mixed Concrete), previously the sponsors of the German golfer, Bernhard Langer, and the British motor racing driver, Kenny Acheson, who picked up the tab.

One of the leading European teams might well have paid lip-service to Doyle's track ambitions, but once the road season was under way they were bound to want to exploit his strength and his race-winning capacity, developed as a pursuiter, to sustain a high pace over the final kilometres – perhaps not in the national tours, since he was not built to be a genuine climber, but certainly in the classics and the shorter stage races. And many thought that was the path he should have taken. But the less demanding home sponsors and the more relaxed domestic programme allowed him to set his own agenda of road races, track meetings and specialised training, which suited his longer-term plans. Not that there was much slack in his

Danny Clark, looking a little care-worn, slings an eager Doyle into the madison at Munich in 1988. They go on to beat the Belgians, Stan Tourné and Etienne De Wilde on points

143

Pursuit and capture: Doyle has the satisfaction of catching the reigning world pursuit champion, Alain Bondue of France, in the European omnium championships at Herning, Denmark, in 1982

summer schedule. In 1982 he won the Girvan stage race for the second time; in 1983 he came second in the international Sealink race, as he did the next year; he rode the Milk Race; and at some time he won stages in all three of those events

Meanwhile Doyle continued his apprenticeship in the Sixes, where, as Webb points out, 'the group who make it to the top have always jealously guarded their positions and been unhelpful to riders on their way up.' Doyle regarded them as sergeant-majors: 'Recruits would look up to these more established riders, and if one of them said jump, or told you off, you'd sit up and take notice.' Sometimes, too, they would stage-manage the action: 'During the afternoon the leader of the Blue Train might say, in the next devil I want so-and-so to win. Maybe because the rider came from that town, or because his sponsor was visiting the track. But it would only happen in the afternoon session. And there'd always be a good reason.' Doyle watched and learnt and tried to assert himself without stepping on too many toes.

Charly Mottet, stage winner and yellow jersey in the Tour de France, is Doyle's partner in the 1986 Paris 6. They finish second to Clark and another celebrated French roadman, Bernard Vallet

Although the Skol track had been dismantled for the last time at Wembley in 1980, Webb, who owned it, took it to other continental sites which lacked a permanent velodrome. At Herning, a town in Jutland with only 55,000 people, he promoted, against all the apparent odds, a highly successful Six which lasted for a decade. This provided Doyle with one sure venue, and gradually he built up his contacts at others until he was regularly, if not fully, employed through the winter. But he was still looking for what even some highly-regarded riders never achieve, a first six-day victory.

The breakthrough came in October 1983 at Berlin, the opening Six of the season. Until then Doyle had been switching partners with almost every event, and although some of these had been highly efficient six-day men, they were not in that top bracket which produced the race-winners. But now, for the first time, he was teamed up with one of the most exciting sprinters and successful riders on the circuit, Danny Clark.

Clark, from Georgetown, Tasmania, has a lot in common with other freebooting Aussie travellers who have come to Europe with their hopes of

145

making a fortune tied together by a shoestring. The difference is that Clark, having made the move almost by accident, succeeded through talent and a cussed determination not to be beaten. He was an outstanding amateur. He was second to Hallam in the pursuit at the 1970 Commonwealth Games, and two years later took the silver medal in the kilometre at the Olympic Games in Munich, also competing in an Australian pursuit team whose main objective was not to ride together but blow each other off the track. And an amateur he might have remained if his father, the Australian coach, hadn't been eased out of the selection process for the 1974 Commonwealth Games. In protest Clark impulsively turned pro two days later.

Having won just about all the pro races that were to be won in Australia, but gained little profit by it, Clark decided to chance his arm in Europe in 1975 and try to break into the Sixes. He alighted in Belgium, rode the *kermesses* to earn his bread and butter, and by the end of the season was working his way towards the top of the class in that painfully hard school. But no six-day contracts came his way.

He got his chance when another rider fell ill just before the start of the Frankfurt 6. With less than 24 hours to prepare, Clark borrowed a track bike from Barry Hoban, a fellow exile in Ghent, plus shorts, wheels and a spare bike from other friendly donors, and reached Frankfurt with an hour or so to spare. He had no mechanic or soigneur. Even then, Sercu, the boss rider at the event, said that Clark would need better wheels than that, and lent him a pair of his own.

The Six got off to a good start, and after three days Clark and his French team-mate Alain Van Lancker were only two laps down. But Van Lancker, winner of six Sixes, was coming to the end of his life on the boards and, feeling unwell, decided to go home, leaving Clark to ride on alone. Clark's response was characteristic. He ignored the laps tally and went for the points instead: 'I just kept winning all the sprints and devils and doing lap records, and that is how I started my Six career.' The promoters were so impressed that he was fitted into a few more events that season, and the following winter, having signed with the Belgian Carlos team for a more secure summer of *kermesses*, he was booked for the whole season.

In 1976–7, too, Clark struck up a partnership with a fellow Australian, Don Allen, who had previously ridden two Tours of France and one of Spain, and had just broken into the Sixes. They were a well-matched pair, especially after they grew identical handlebar moustaches to mark their

Cabin talk between Doyle and his partner, Eric Vanderaerden, at Antwerp in 1987. At the age of 21, this precocious Dutch roadman-sprinter had already won the yellow jersey in the 1983 Tour de France, but in a decade of professional racing he has ridden few Sixes. On this rare occasion he and Doyle came third

corporate identity and won 15 Sixes together. But at the end of the 1982–3 season, Allen returned to Australia to open a business, and Clark was looking for another regular partner.

At first sight Clark and Doyle, the rough and the smooth, were not an obvious pairing. Doyle was, and remains, a romantic, very much in love with the bicycle and in particular with the glamour and applause of the winter tracks. Not averse to the money they earn him, of course, but still enjoying the racing for its own sake. Clark was outwardly more cynical. He found training tedious, and said he was sick of racing; he was in it to support his wife and family and put enough by to start a business of his own back home. Two years before he had told Doyle: 'I'd rather live in Australia and have a bit of life before the Russians get there.'

He was then 30, and gave himself only another few years in the game: 'There is no way I would ride until I was 37, like Sercu.' He'd only do that if he was a European; 'what else have they got to do?' he asked with typical Aussie disdain. And yet in 1991–2, now 40 and having just recorded his 65th win – so joining Peter Post in third place in the all-time rankings – he was still riding most of the Sixes. And although this was supposed to be his retirement season, he still seemed distinctly reluctant to leave the stage.

Yet despite the differences in their nature, Clark and Doyle hit it off. They spoke the same language, of course. They both had a single-minded rage to win whenever they saw the chance. And their particular talents complemented each other: Clark with his electrifying sprint and Doyle with his sustained strength raising the tempo in the chases on the far side of the track.

Doyle had been confident that if he were teamed with one of the recognised leaders he would be in contention. But he also realised that he was on trial in Berlin, and with Clark as his tutor, he rode single-mindedly to prove his case. The result was in doubt until two minutes from the end, when they were on the same lap as the Danish team Frank Oersted and the 25 points at stake in the final sprint between Clark and Gert Frank were more than the margin between them. It was winner-take-all, and the winner was Clark. Doyle's was the first Six victory for a British rider since Tony Gowland's at Wembley in 1972, the first on the Continent since Tom Simpson's at Brussels in 1965, and the first ever in Germany.

A week later, with a repeat victory win over the same opponents at Dortmund, Doyle became the first Brit to win twice in modern six-day racing. But more important than that, he established himself in the eyes of promoters as a leading actor in the sport, not just one of the supporting players. But there the run ended. The next Six was at Frankfurt, and although Doyle was keen to keep up the momentum, and so was the promoter to book this new winning combination, he turned down the invitation. The event had a reputation for crashes, and having got so far

Doyle didn't want injury to bring him to a stop. Clark accepted, and on the second night he did crash, breaking his hip.

Clark's recovery was remarkably quick. Within three months he was making his comeback at Rotterdam, with Doyle again at his side. But he was still walking with a stick, and although he could cycle, it was not with his old strength. Rather than treating him leniently, the other riders made it even harder for the pair of them. 'They knew he was suffering and going through hell,' says Doyle, 'but they showed no generosity. He'd made their legs ache before the crash, and now they were doing the same to him.' They finished seventh, 15 laps down, and the only consolation for Doyle was being able to take some of the strain himself, and so repay a little of what he owed Clark for his rising fortunes.

Otherwise Doyle rode through much of that winter with another good Australian, Gary Wiggins, with whom he won the European madison championship in 1984 and began to form a fairly regular pairing. They had five fourth places, and a second at Bremen, and the following year had their only victory, again at Bremen, beating the favourites, Clark and the most popular of all post-war German stars, Dietrich Thurau. The promoters seemed to have lost interest in the interrupted partnership of Clark and Doyle, although it was occasionally revived in 1985–6 to bring further victories at Maastricht and Copenhagen. And then, over the next three winters, it came back into fashion and went from one peak to another.

In the autumn of 1986 they repeated their original successes, snapping up Berlin and Dortmund in turn. Doyle then went on to win the third Six of the season, at Grenoble, but this time in company with Francesco Moser, the one man who gave Italian cycling its credibility at this period. And since Copenhagen had been the last Six of the previous season, Doyle had produced a run of four victories, which was exceptional even in the honours list of a Sercu or a Post.

In the next year they twice finished second before clicking again at Maastricht, but by the time the winter ended had also notched up Bremen, Rotterdam and Paris. But it was during 1988–9 that their position was finally confirmed as the most voracious combination on the circuit. In seven outings together they came away with the bouquets from five events: Münster, Berlin, Dortmund (in succession), Munich and Cologne. It was at that point that the promoters, under increasing pressure from rival riders and their sponsors, decided that enough was enough.

They were given no rides together in the following season, which anyway was cut short for Doyle by his crash at Munich. And since then they have only occasionally been reunited. All the same, on one of these occasions – Doyle's return to Munich in 1990 – they won for the 19th time. It was a record that outstripped all their contemporaries and had been achieved only twice in the past – by the Belgian team of Rik Van Steenbergen and Emile

Severeyns in the mid-1960s, and by Peter Post (Hol) and Fritz Pfenninger (Swi) early in the 1970s. There is little doubt that if Clark and Doyle had been allowed to choose each other as partners as often as they wished, they would have added substantially to that figure.

What stopped them was the system of autocratic rule by the six-day promoters, who are not only the impresarios of their events but their own team selectors. To what extent they manipulate other aspects of the racing is matter of conjecture, but the right to pair the riders at their own discretion already gives them the power to dictate which riders will be in contention. In general they do this to attract the crowds. They may decide, for instance, that this aim is best served by putting on an evenly balanced race between six to eight teams which will keep up the suspense until the final hours, in which case they will split up, not team up, the strongest riders. Or they may want to contrive a popular home win by putting the local hero with the strongest man in the race and diluting the power of the remaining teams. Or, having signed an expensive star from the road-racing world, they may want to make sure he gets a safe passage by assigning an experienced, top-rank rider to act as his guide. Or they may choose to do this for a promising new rider whom they want to bring on.

Doyle, not only a proven winner but a steady, reliable rider with a friendly manner, has been particularly vulnerable to this kind of sporting compromise. When not riding with Clark he has often been given the job of 'taxi-driver', and has had some pretty distinguished passengers in the back of his cab. He rode twice with Francesco Moser, an idol of his, whom he had watched take his world road race title in Venezuela in 1977 – nine years later winning at Grenoble with him. He guided Greg LeMond through his only Six in the autumn of 1988, when the American was struggling to regain form and reputation after his hunting accident the year before. Twice he came within an ace of winning with the Dubliner, Stephen Roche. And the German, Dietrich Thurau, had paid him the compliment of saying that he wished he had found Doyle as a partner earlier in his career. But although these memories offer some compensation, more often acting as chauffeur to the great has cost him any realistic chance of victory.

It was more difficult to split up Clark and Allen, since they formed a national team, and an Australia *v* Germany contest has a certain crowd appeal. But there is no such impediment to the divorce of an Australian and an Englishman, and there is little they can do to avoid being separated. Sometimes Doyle takes this hard, seeing the loss of opportunities to add to his 23 wins. More often he is 'philosophical': 'Obviously the more established riders will be taken into the promoter's confidence to discuss the formation of the teams, but it's the promoter who has the final say.'

No rider is in a better position than Doyle to sway the decision. Nowadays he is the *seigneur*, the boss, chosen by the riders of the Blue Train – ahead of the undiplomatic Clark or the volatile Etienne De Wilde – to represent them in dealings with the management. But even he can't buck the system: 'If you don't like the terms they offer, you can take them or leave them. And often it will be spelt out as bluntly as that. The promoters know they are holding the ace because there are scores of guys begging for an opportunity to race. They've got you by the short and curlies, and some of them like to flex their muscles.'

A slightly sinister development, too, is the increased pressure from the trade team sponsors. This has intensified since Fédération Internationale de Cyclisme Professionel (FICP) points were introduced into six-day racing during 1990–1. The FICP is the governing body of professional cycling, and the points are awarded to individual riders according to their finishing positions in certain major races. The number of points accumulated by the riders in a trade team then determines whether or not it is accepted for further events. In the 1992 Tour de France, for instance, the first 16 teams on the FICP points table were automatically accepted. Only six 'wild card' teams were added to the field according to the potential their riders displayed after the Tour of Italy and the Dauphiné stage race had been run. So the FICP points earned on the winter tracks now have considerable bearing on the teams' summer programmes. The team sponsors do not want their six-day men to lose points by being paired with weaker riders. And those sponsors have economic muscles of their own to flex.

On the whole Doyle, however much he may inwardly seethe, goes along with the system and rarely speaks out publicly against it; he sees no alternative. But in an interview he gave to *Cycling Weekly* in January 1992, some of those frustrations boiled over. He complained that he and Clark had ridden as a team only three times that season, while other top pairings like Andreas Kappes and Etienne De Wilde had been kept together for the past three winters. He believed that Kappes, a big box-office draw in Germany, had the promoters there in his pocket. But he also saw the influence of their trade team, Telekom, in the fact that normally their partnership remained intact even in the Belgian Sixes. Doyle was picked with De Wilde at Ghent only because Kappes was taking a rest after his hard ride in Munich.

'With hindsight,' says Doyle, 'Danny and I may have done more harm than good when we won those five Sixes in 88–89. But you have to make the most of you chances while you can.'

A winter's tale 9

The third German Six in a row, and the fifth and last of the season, was at Stuttgart. Of the other seven staged in 1991–2, two were in Belgium, two in France, and one each in Switzerland, USSR and Denmark. When you consider that the Moscow 6 was really organised from Bremen, this meant German control over half the season's events. This is curiously out of proportion with Germany's small impact on professional road racing in the summer, which in any case comes mainly from riders like Olaf Ludwig and Uwe Ampler, brought up in the old German Democratic Republic.

Six-day racing is its speciality, and the Stuttgart 6 is in the national tradition of Pilsner, ox roasts and hard racing. The track at the Schleyer-Halle is 285m, the biggest in regular use in Sixes (unless, of course, Moscow is repeated). Doyle reckoned that in one madison chase the previous year, he and his partner, Urs Freuler, had to circle it 70 times, covering nearly 20km, before they gained a lap. This time he was teamed for a second time with the Australian, Dean Woods.

STUTTGART 6

Thursday, 16 January

Well, Gianni Bugno, the world road race champion, has made his six-day debut. Obviously he was very apprehensive, but he was able to adapt much better because of the large track. Like a lot of road riders, he finds this and the Antwerp 6 ideal preparation for the forthcoming road season. Bugno's partner, for instance, is Guido Bontempi of the Carrera team, and other roadmen here are Ad Wijnands of TVM, Pete Pieters (Tulip), Laurenzo Lapage (Isoglass) – plus the regular six-day roadmen like Etienne De Wilde, Andreas Kappes and Remig Stumpf. The race director now is Roman Hermann, who rode nearly 200 Sixes, winning 15 of them and retiring only three years ago.

Friday, 17 January

The second night being Friday, a good crowd. And with a 75km chase in which a new track record average speed of 54.9kph was set, a lot of guys were swimming. Pieters, who is Urs Freuler's partner, is suffering from a stomach bug, and we wonder if he will be able to finish the Six.

Bugno, though, was a lot more at ease and I am sure that, given time, he will be able to adapt to a life on the boards. The size of the track makes it really difficult to take laps, so the racing becomes very tactical.

Saturday, 18 January

The Halle was full to capacity with 12,000 spectators for the Golden Night. The highlight of the evening was provided by Michael Hübner, a darling of the German public who won his second successive world keiren title on this track last August. He made an attack on the world 500m flying start and broke the record with 27.35 sec against the 27.41 sec of the Australian, Stephen Pate. It was ironical because in the 1991 world sprint championships here, Pate took the bronze medal only to be disqualified after a positive drug test. For the whole evening a great atmosphere again and a hard programme, with a 75km and a 30 min chase as well as all the trimmings. Racing went on from 7.40 pm to 2.30 am.

Sunday, 19 January

After starting at 2 pm we had an early finish at 7.30 pm to look forward to. I was obviously motivated by having my good friend and derny driver, Paul Wingrave, coming over to support me. So I had to win the big chase to keep him happy!

The afternoon was devoted to the kids, with McDonalds sponsoring the programme and Roland McDonald playing a major role. The kids are the spectators of the future, so it's important to placate them and their parents.

It was nice to be able to relax for the evening, change into civvies and to go a restaurant in town for a meal with my soigneur, Pierrot. We really are spoilt.

Monday, 20 January

It's Carnival Night and racing stops from 9.30 to 10.30 pm for a big procession and a show. Last year's carnival was cancelled because of the war in the Middle East, so it made a welcome comeback. Pieters and Werner Stutz were forced to retire due to illness. There is a virus floating around and giving riders backdoor trots, temperatures, etc. Also the track here is very cold and draughty. I felt rough so I made sure I rested as much as possible during the day. I ate very carefully, kept very warm and wrapped up well on the track. My condition is obviously superb as once on the bike I felt and showed no side-effects.

Clark and Bincoletto are riding very well and look poised for victory, but with the final night's programme being so hard, nothing is certain. We will be starting with balustrade sprints, a 30 min chase, team devil and derny racing – which counts on the gen class now, which means that laps are won and lost. Then more sprints, a points race and a 75km chase to round off the Six. So there's no promenade on the final day.

153

Tuesday, 21 January

The six-day season is starting to take its toll now, with Remig Stumpf as well as Stutz having to retire; Stumpf apparently had a sore foot. This meant that two new teams had to be formed.

Danny and Binco went on to victory in a thrilling finale where all the riders knew that they had been in a hell of a race. A crowd of 10,000 watched the last night's racing.

The riders have been sleeping in a hotel nearby, but the living quarters for the personnel are reminiscent of Cardboard City. My soigneur and runner are being forced to sleep on a mattress on the floor – no blankets, sheets or pillows provided. Can you imagine the masseurs or trainers of Boris Becker or Ivan Lendl sleeping on the floor in the changing rooms at Wimbledon? Consequently throughout the week the personnel were referred to as 'the tramps' – in jest but with an element of truth.

My form throughout has been very good – proved by the fact that during the 50-lap points race I lapped the field alone and went on to win a trophy as the best rider throughout the points race. Bugno survived to finish and earned the respect of his fellow pros. I was impressed by his politeness and the way he had his feet on the floor, unlike a lot of far less talented so-called professionals.

Overall the promoters were delighted by a very good press and TV coverage, increased crowd attendance and worthy winners. I'll be glad to be sitting in an airbus on the runway at eight tomorrow morning and heading home for a couple of days. I will be able to catch up with all the important things that have been going on in my absence, like what's been happening in Coronation Street.

Result: 1 Danny Clark (Australia)/Pierangelo Bincoletto (It), 362pts; 2 Tourné (Bel)/Veggerby (Den), 283pts; 3 Kappes (Ger)/De Wilde (Bel), 325pts, at one lap; 8 Doyle (GB)/Woods (Australia), 186pts, at 6 laps

Chapter 10

Crock of gold

After Doyle's precocious triumph at Besançon, it was four years before he won another medal in the world pursuit championships, and six before he regained his title. But he is nothing if not a methodical rider, who prepares assiduously, plans ahead and learns from his mistakes. Even as he twice failed by the narrowest of margins to gain a place in the first three, and twice came away with silver medals from the final, he developed a systematic approach which was to lift him back on top of the world at Colorado in 1986, and the next year put him into a position at Ghent where only the most perverse bad luck would deny him a third title.

Through no fault of his own, or anyone else's, Doyle was unable to defend his rainbow jersey at Brno in 1981. The day before he was due to fly out to Czechoslovakia for the world championships he went to Herne Hill for a final training session with Paul Wingrave, who paced him on a derny around the big concrete track.

I was going very fast, probably 40mph, and virtually touching the mudguard in front of me, when the derny misfired. I was too close to go round it, and as it coughed and spluttered I came down, sliding along on my backside for 25–30yds. I completely skinned it. Even then, although I was obviously in pain and discomfort, I didn't take the injury too seriously at the time. I wasn't due to race in the qualifying round for maybe another six days, so I reckoned I had time to get over it. Paul and the park-keeper at the stadium cleaned me up as best they could, and I went home and got the wound dressed again. Unfortunately the next day an infection set in, I developed a temperature, and there was no way I could go.

This was particularly galling for Doyle. He knew he was in good form, having only recently travelled to Denmark to beat Hans-Henrik Oersted, one of his strongest challengers, in a pursuit match on his own home track. Now he had to stay at home while Oersted took the silver medal in Brno, losing only to the Frenchman, Alain Bondue, in the final. 'I'm not saying I would have won the title,' says Doyle, 'but I feel I would at least have come home with a medal.'

The following year, 1982, brought another disappointment, all the more keenly felt because the world championships were held in England – the track events at Leicester and the road races at Goodwood. After missing Brno the previous year, there was heavy pressure on Doyle to prove that the 1980 result had been no fluke, and the tension increased when less than a month before the world's he lost his national title to Sean Yates, the man whom the press had cast as the perpetual stone in his shoe. It was the first time for six years that Doyle had not been either amateur or pro champion.

When the same Saffron Lane track was transformed into a world arena later in the month Doyle still couldn't break the spell. Although he set the fastest time of the series in the quarter-finals, a British record of 5 min 53.5 sec, he was beaten in the next round by the reigning champion, Bondue, who went on to confirm his title. And in the ride off for third and fourth he lost to the Italian, Bidinost, by a fraction of a second. So he came fourth – 'the worst place to finish because it's so close'.

The following week he competed at Goodwood in the road race for the first and last time, and with nothing to lose found it thoroughly relaxing. He covered 145 miles 'and really enjoyed it', dropping out not because he was tired but because there was no point in finishing 15 minutes behind in 50th place. Better to wander to the finish and watch a magnificent sprint in which Guiseppe Saronni saw off some young American called Greg LeMond and the more familiar figure of Sean Kelly. 'As a professional you've got to live to fight another day.'

This he did in Zurich in 1983, where again he finished the pursuit in fourth place, and again lost in the semi-finals to the eventual champion, Steele Bishop of Australia. His long-time opponent, Oersted, then beat him in the ride-off for third and fourth. On the whole Doyle was better pleased with his first appearance in the 50km pro points race. There was little doubt that Urs Freuler would win, as he had for the past two years. He was riding in his own country, had already taken the keirin title and, not to put too fine a point on it, had his support well organised. But Doyle rode aggressively, and although in the face of the combines he finished only fifth, he felt he had made a match of it.

In 1984 at Barcelona and 1985 in Bassano, Doyle got back on the podium with silver medals, in each case beaten by Oersted in the final. At Bassano in particular he felt he had acquitted himself well, for all four semi-finalists had been world champions – the other two were the German bronze medallist, Gregor Braun, who had previously held the title in 1977 and 1978, and Francesco Moser, fourth, who had won in 1976 – and the standard of the riding was unusually high. All the same, there remained the final leap to the top step of the podium, and Doyle set that as his target for the following year.

It was at Bassano that Mick Bennett, a member of the highly successful British pursuit team of the early 1970s, and later a professional rider on road and track, entered into the story. Doyle was still a member of the junior squad when Bennett first came across him at a Herne Hill track meeting, and Bennett remembers him as 'a long, lanky lad, quite ungainly on the bike', but certainly a trier. 'He was in a break with Ian Hallam and me and we worked him over. But because he finished third, I know I went over afterwards to Harry Walker, the Welsh masseur who was managing the junior team, and said that he was going to be a good lad, Doyle.'

For a few years he saw little of Doyle, who was working his way up through the amateur ranks; he next noticed him in the Skol 6, where Doyle was riding one of those 'revenge' matches much favoured by promoters, against Bert Oosterbosch, the Dutchman he had beaten for the world title at Grenoble a few weeks before. 'He was very, very serious about it, but I thought to myself that Peter Post [the race director at Wembley] would want Oosterbosch to win it, which he did.'

After that, Doyle having turned pro, Bennett found himself riding the criteriums and road races with him week by week. But it didn't bring them any closer: 'We seemed to be constantly at one another.' But in 1983 Doyle was asked to bring a combined British team to the Etoile des Espoires stage race in France and invited Bennett to join it: 'He was organising people and sorting them out even then.'

Bennett recalls that the team went off in two cars, arriving in the village where they had been booked in at two or three in the morning. But although Doyle had the address written down, they couldn't find it. 'I know what we'll do,' said Tony. 'You all stand in the village square, and I'll go and find a coin box and phone the number. Then when you hear it ringing, wherever it is, we'll know that's the place.' 'Already coming up with these bright ideas,' says Bennett, 'And you know, it worked.'

A week or so after that, in October 1983, Bennett had a motor accident in France which ended his cycling career and destroyed his plans for the future. Much of the next year, too, was lost in the process of rehabilitation. He already had a bike shop in Birmingham which had occupied his spare energy while he was still riding. But when, in the autumn of 1984, Alan Rushton offered him something more substantial in the way of a job in London, working in sports management and promotion, he accepted.

By this time he and Doyle were getting on reasonably well, 'but only as one pro with another'. So he was surprised, and touched, when one day Doyle rang up to suggest that instead of staying in digs in London and driving back to the Midlands at weekends, he should come and live with Anne and himself in a spare room at their house at Ashford.

157

He took up the invitation and remained with them for 18 months, in the process becoming increasingly involved in Doyle's career. He began training him behind a moped on the roads around Ashford, Staines and Windsor – 'amazing sessions going along at up to 60 miles an hour'. Bennett, who had begun to manage the British pro team at world championships, also worked with Doyle at Bassano in 1985, identifying the weaknesses in his approach and the areas which could do with improvement. Then followed 'a very intense period', leading up to the championships in Colorado Springs the following summer, when the two of them devised a detailed programme of self-improvement for Doyle which, they were both convinced, would enable him to win back his pursuit title.

Doyle had made a considerable, if sometimes puzzling, impression upon Bennett. He had this fastidious, almost clinical approach to his profession. He was very serious about his preparations. At the same time he was a highly social person. There would be people coming constantly to the house, which was always kept extremely presentable. He was highly aware of how it looked. And then, in the middle of all this activity, Bennett was staggered to find Doyle coming in late at night splattered with paint, which he explained away only when Bennett pointedly asked him. Doyle, as described earlier, was doing up Alf Whiteway's house. Bennett couldn't get over it. 'I thought, for a bloke in the middle of his preparations for the world's ... well, Oersted wouldn't be doing that.'

So came the time to leave for the United States. Bennett remembers:

He always used to do his own thing, book his own travel, organise his own hotel – wherever the British Cycling Federation *weren't* staying. He realised that they made blunders, like hanging around too long in airport lounges, or finding that the hotel wasn't to their liking, too noisy or whatever.

I went with him, and he liked this idea. It's almost as if he wants the family, *his* family, whether or not they are relatives, around him. There was always Pierrot de Wit and Geoff Cooke and myself close to him at the world's, and he could be very demanding. I think he wants that emotional attachment. One side of him is this independent traveller, who goes anywhere, makes his own arrangements. But at the end of it he wants this link with home and his nearest friends. I don't think he can go long without this, and I think it's a lovely quality to have.

Dead to the world, but not asleep. Doyle gets his mind attuned before the world pursuit championships in Barcelona

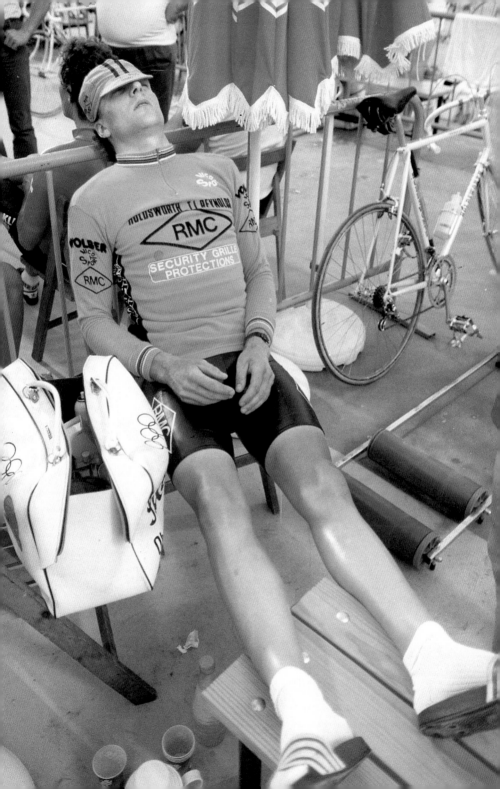

*A final word with Mick Bennett
who holds him at the start line . . .*

. . . and he's away

Certainly it's rare enough in professional cycling, particularly on the Continent, though there is one champion who shares it, Greg LeMond. In the Tour de France, where riders have traditionally cut themselves off from their families as though they were serving a four-week custodial sentence, LeMond likes to know that his wife and children and parents, better still the whole clan, while out of sight are near at hand if he needs them.

Bennett believed that Doyle should prepare for the championships as his pursuit squad had done 15 years before – that is, in privacy, without distractions, 'keeping the whole team shrouded in mystery'. Everything had to be done according to format, even in the period prior to the competition. Work out on the rollers 20 minutes, rub down 5 minutes, and so on.

He admits the approach was very blinkered and demanding on everyone else around:

> Those on the periphery had to do it how we wanted it to be done. There had to be no-one in the cabin, just me and the soigneur and Tony. Anyone who even dared to knock on the door would be chastised for it. It was a closed, cosseted environment, very much of the sort that surrounds a boxer until the moment he comes into the ring. But that's the way Tony liked it, and it seemed to work.

Doyle had prefaced his trip to America by regaining the national pursuit title, which in the last few years he had not contested because of a clash of dates. Now riding what the *Daily Mail* described as his £4,500 superbike – the cost of the carbon-fibre wheels accounting for more than half of that: ' "a bargain", says Doyle' – he confirmed that his Leicester form had held up as he trained at altitude in the 7-Eleven velodrome at Colorado Springs. The only blip came two days before the qualifying round, when he was bitten in the calf by a police dog as he was leaving the track after an early morning work-out. Not any dog but, as the local papers dutifully recorded, a Belgian malinois called D-Jaggo. Its handler had given it too much rope, distracted, he said, by the activities of a Japanese camera crew.

No stitches were needed, but the bite caused pain and bruising, plus the risk of infection, at a delicate stage in Doyle's preparations. And to complicate matters the team had to decide whether or not he should have the anti-tetanus jab which was a routine precaution in such cases. Bennett was against it: 'If we subject Tony to a test, and the results are positive,' he told the *Colorado Springs Gazette Telegraph*, 'he will be telling himself he is not up to par, and psychologically this will be unnerving.' Doyle didn't want any fuss either, though it was a relief to him that a doctor friend of his, Andy Coady, was on hand to look at the wound and say it wasn't serious. 'Somebody else would have made a great commotion,' says Bennett, 'It would have totally destroyed their confidence. Tony just took it in his stride,

161

almost made a joke of it. I still had the worry that he might have rabies or something, but he just brushed it off.'

This was Doyle's other self, which offered relief from what seemed his solemn, almost obsessive preoccupation with his own physical and mental well-being. 'In fact they were good times,' says Bennett. 'After the serious day Tony would relax and have a laugh. He was always looking for the funny side. Even when his mind was on his work he'd store things up and bring them out later. And then you'd think, well, he's hasn't really got a one-track mind, he does notice these other things.'

The incident with the dog was quickly forgotten, and from there on everything went smoothly. He put up a personal best in the qualifying round, caught the Belgian, Jean-Luc Vandenbroucke, in the 12th lap of the quarter-finals, and in the semis set a world best time of 5 min 40.338 sec in beating the Dane, Jesper Worre. So for the third year running the final was to be between himself and Oersted. But the champion already knew that his own fastest qualifying time of 5-40.622 had been beaten by an opponent who this year seemed to be in irresistible form.

The final, held on the cool, still evening of the same day before a sell-out crowd of 8,200, was less a battle of speed than of wits between two old rivals who knew each other's strengths and habits only too well. Oersted was normally a slow starter, winding up the pace as the pursuit proceeded. But this time, wanting to surprise Doyle, he sped away from the gun, covering the first kilometre in 1-11.05, almost a second faster than Doyle. Nor did he relent, for after 4km with one to go, he had a lead of almost two seconds. This put him roughly 30 metres ahead, and it seemed to almost everyone at the track that in another three laps' time the Dane would take his third successive title.

Bennett, though, knew from the evidence of earlier rounds that Doyle was riding his finishing lap a second faster than Oersted. It was simply a question of whether Doyle could retrieve the other second before that.

Doyle's fight back began on the 13th lap of the 333.3m track, and at the bell he had cut the lead back to 0.36 sec. Oersted, unable to respond, now knew that his tactics had failed, and the crowd at last recognised that they were witnessing one of the most dramatic counter-attacks ever staged in the world pro pursuit championships. Turning in a final kilometre of 1-5.91, Doyle swept through to win by a margin almost identical to his earlier deficit: 1.946 sec.

The British camp was overjoyed. 'Everybody from the BCF wanted to jump on the bandwagon,' says Bennett, 'and Tony went along with it. He felt he had to, it was good PR, but in a way he just wanted to share it with the people he was close to, the ones who were around him.'

The celebrations didn't stop there. On his return home to Gatwick, Doyle found a reception party of 50 people, led by Malcolm Jarvis, managing

162

director of Amoco, one of his sponsors, waiting at the airport. Staff from another sponsor, Ever Ready, were also there in force. So were his family and friends. And that weekend, when for the first time the streets of Westminster were closed for a Kellogg's city centre race, Doyle was first across the line in his rainbow jersey, beating another world champion, Hennie Kuiper, in the sprint.

Vienna, 1987, was a let-down, even if Doyle did come away from the Ferry-Dusika stadium with two medals. It had become clear over the past couple of years that Doyle and Oersted were so equally matched in ability that victory was likely to go to whichever of them reached the last four of the pursuit in peak condition. In this case Doyle peaked too soon. He had got himself ready with his usual single-mindedness. But he was tired after a hard winter and a heavy promotional programme. This is a demand which many world champions find it hard to resist, and in Doyle's case had included a personal racing appearance in Danny Clark's homeland, Tasmania. As Bennett frankly admitted in Vienna, 'He was over the top five weeks ago.'

He had been persuaded, with difficulty, to take a week's rest – 'We almost had to cage him up to achieve that' – but he couldn't reproduce the urgent tempo of Colorado Springs. With no great difficulty he outclassed Oosterbosch to reach the pursuit semi-finals, but there he found himself drawn against the old enemy. He also suffered the indignity of being caught by Oersted in the 13th of 20 laps. In the end he had to settle for bronze by once again beating Vandenbroucke in the final for third and fourth.

The year before he had ridden the points race on the day after the pursuit final, but only to lend support to his British team-mate, Shaun Wallace. This time he rode it in earnest, taking on almost single-handed that third or so of the 25-man field which was blatantly riding against him and for the benefit of Freuler, who had now held the title since 1981. Although closely marked, Doyle stayed level on points with Freuler right up to the bell so that the championship hung on the last sprint to the line. With the door slammed in his face by blocking opponents, Doyle could not stop Freuler taking yet another gold medal, but his own silver, added to the pursuit bronze, was no mean reward for a tired rider who had inadvertantly passed his best-by date.

Doyle recalls the 1988 world championships at Ghent as the year he made a gift of the title: 'I wasn't beaten, I gave it away.' The recipient was a Polish rider, Lech Piasecki, with better credentials on the road than the track. Winner of the world amateur road race in Italy in 1985, he had been one of the first East European stars allowed to take up a professional career in the West, and had made a name for himself as a nippy time triallist and a shrewd opportunist. The previous year in the Tour de France he had used both qualities snatch the yellow jersey on the opening day. Again at Ghent, though not in the same class as a pursuiter, he was quick enough to exploit an abnormal spell of disarray in the Doyle camp and this time make the rainbow jersey his. He might even agree with Doyle's overall verdict, for although he continued to ride the road races he never returned to contest the world pursuit.

To Bennett it was the year when the systematic approach, backed by a comprehensive support group, reached its zenith. It had paid off handsomely at Colorado Springs, and was thought not to have failed so much as miscued in Vienna. Now the camp was further augmented, and Bennett says, 'With hindsight there were obviously too many people there, too many different psychologies involved, too many personalities.' Although the blunder which threw Doyle's preparations into turmoil just before the final, one panic leading to another, was no direct fault of Bennett's, he, as the overall manager, accepted the ultimate blame. 'I should have recognised the flaws in the set-up.'

'That year I was very serious and very determined about my approach,' says Doyle. 'I had really got myself right in my method of training, and how I was planning things. I'd been well organised before, but I'm always looking for ways to improve myself.' Ghent, as he knew from his experience in the Sixes, was well worth the extra effort since it would attract the support of a large contingent of British bikies. There was also the practical matter that the indispensable De Wit lived conveniently close by in Brussels. All the omens looked right.

As usual Doyle had taken charge of the accommodation, going off to Ghent six weeks in advance with De Wit and his mechanic, Bob Arnold, to look at the hotel and the newly-built 250m outdoor wooden track. At the Hotel Astrid in Aalst he made sure he had the quietest bedroom, sorted out storage for the bikes and equipment, discussed with the chef the kind of meals he wanted and when he would want them. Then he checked how long it took him to drive himself to the track, both on the motorway and the side roads. Nothing apparently was left to chance.

The additional recruits to the team – beyond that Vienna nucleus of mechanic and soigneur, Bennett himself and his assistant, Geoff Cooke, and Dr Coady, who had been in Colorado with them – were a sports psychologist (Ian Maynard), a sports physiologist (Peter Keen) and a derny driver (Paul Wingrave), who doubled as a minder at the track. Ah yes, and there was Mark Shaw from the Rushton office, who operated the video camera. Everything was videoed, from the preparation in the cabin to the riding on the track (and, having never seen anything like it before, people began videoing them as they videoed themselves). Not only that, they dressed in the same white overalls at work, sat down to eat in identical tee-shirts, wore matching leisure suits; they were a source of wonder at the track.

The physiologist introduced a new approach to riding the pursuit which,

Ring of confidence: Doyle, in his rainbow jersey, is back home to celebrate his second world pro pursuit title won at Colorado Springs in 1986. Sharing his pleasure are Dr Andy Coady and, wearing the gold medal, Mick Bennett

looking back, Bennett now considers 'almost too clinical, too text-book'. But the lead-up, which had begun as early as May, was very much on the methodical lines that the team had already practised. Before arriving in Belgium, for instance, Doyle had been asked to consider and respond in writing to a series of hypothetical questions which the team called, 'What Ifs?':

1 The weather in Belgium is so bad that the quality of my training is low?
2 I find myself becoming easily tired during the championships?
3 I find from the first day out in Belgium my bodyweight is decreasing?
4 The short trip from the hotel to the velodrome is taking much longer than it should because of traffic problems?
5 I find myself distracted by an official who seems preoccupied with my bicycle?
6 I feel that Mick is spending too much time on private business?

7 The mechanic is never around when I need him?

8 There is nothing to do in Ghent?

9 We learn that we have limited access to the competition circuit for training/practice purposes?

10 I am getting worried about the event days ahead – which is causing me to lose sleep?

11 I am forced to give a Press Conference which I don't really want to know about as soon as I arrive in Belgium?

12 After another poor performance in the National Pursuit Championships I am experiencing lots of self doubt? [This last eventuality did not arise because Doyle won his fifth title, catching his opponent in the semis and the final.]

Doyle's build-up was programmed month by month, and broken down under such titles as racing commitments, general road work, quality road work, track and simulator, and psychological training aimed at building up confidence and controlling tension. The simulated work at Herne Hill, for instance, included standing-start rides against imagined opponents. 'I'd tell him how good the other rider was,' says Bennett, 'and who it was, Oersted maybe. And I'd say, if I see you look across at him I'll kick you all round the track.' Doyle had to respond solely to Bennett's signals to hold it, speed up a touch and finally, let's have him.

Once the team were installed in Belgium the schedules – typed up and distributed to all the team – became even more detailed and precise. 'Right down to when I was driving him to the track,' says Bennett,

we would have the windows down and we'd be playing Land of Hope and Glory. Inspirational music playing out of the car. I would not question this psychological thing. I thought it was fantastic and very worthwhile. But at the end of the day what broke it down was a personality clash.

Anyway, we had this set routine where there was always a car waiting out on the road in case it was wanted. It was almost stopwatch stuff: you know, blow your nose, sit down, go for a piss. And there were always the same people in the room with Tony: the psychologist and the soigneur and myself, nobody else.

But this meant shutting out people who were not only as felt they had their own special relationship with Doyle, but also something to contribute at that stage. The physiologist, for instance, wanted a wider involvement, and asked why he should be excluded from the dressing room.

Nor was it only members of the Doyle camp – essential to the whole operation but not needed at that moment – who were kept away in case they caused distractions. None of the official BCF party was allowed into the cabin at all. The track was checked before training sessions to see that the coast was clear, and the bike was kept covered whenever Doyle wasn't riding it. They wanted to keep everything to themselves.

In most cases this was simply what Doyle wanted, 'and if Tony wanted X,Y,Z, Tony got X,Y,Z'. But Bennett wasn't going to argue that point with anyone; the orders came from him, and if they weren't prepared to do what he told them, he made it clear that they wouldn't be allowed to stay with the team. In some cases these orders were accepted grudgingly, and Bennett is honest enough to admit that he expressed himself aggressively at times. 'But that was the way I wanted it doing, and that was it. We'd come to win a world title, not make friends and influence people.'

If tensions were mounting, they did not impinge on Doyle, who was really flying; he was, he says, psyched up not only to win but to win in style. And but for the final mishap these tensions might never have come to the surface. Oersted was absent, having decided that his third gold medal at Vienna would do as a retirement present. So it was his Danish heir, Worre, who lined up against Doyle in the qualifying round. And since Worre had been widely tipped to come through as his opponent in the final, Doyle's confidence was boosted by a 6 sec win in which he set the fastest time of the round with 5-49.45. This brought him a quarter-final draw against the slowest qualifier, Michael Grenda of Australia, whom he caught before going on to turn in a remarkably consistent 5-49.38, again the fastest.

A reassuring Tuesday, then, and an even better start to Wednesday's concluding rounds when he met Daniel Wyder in the semi-final. Waving to the crowd, he caught the Swiss in 3-42 after only 3.1km, a near-perfect warm-up for the final later that evening. Piasecki, who went on to knock out Worre in the second semi-final, was going well, especially for a man who had never ridden the world track championships before. But his best time was 5-50.04 in the quarter-final, and unless he pulled out something special, Doyle, simply by maintaining his form, seemed certain to take back the title. Barring accidents, of course. And alas for Doyle, there was not just an accident but a pile-up waiting for him round the next corner. The 'What If?' in this case was, What if the programme is altered without anyone telling me? And no answer had been prepared for that one.

There was no massage cabin for the British team at the track, and Doyle's was at a sports centre about a kilometre away. Knowing that this would be the case, he had issued the members of his own team with two-way radios so that they could keep in touch. Since the cabin had concrete walls they were not particularly reliable. But no matter: a fit man could run the distance between track and cabin in three or four minutes, or cycle it in half that time. All of which makes the evening's happenings all the harder to understand.

Bennett and the inner circle had drawn up a schedule for Tony based on the programme which the organisers had put out the night before; all the team had a copy. So at the appropriate time the psychologist was

167

preparing Doyle in the cabin. Bennett:

> He did it by lying Tony down and relaxing him, which was excellent, after which Tony would change into his skinsuit. All the other people had left the cabin and gone to the track, and I was always telling them to keep us updated with any eventualities – if the programme was brought forward, or back, or whatever. And earlier we had been told, wrongly as it turned out, that it was running 10 minutes late.

No further word came back, and Doyle changed into his skinsuit and went on with the accustomed ritual, unaware that in fact the programme had been brought forward. The first those in the cabin knew of it was when, halfway through Doyle's mental preparation, Paul Wingrave banged on the door, like a theatre call-boy, to say 'Quick, quick, you're on, you're on.'

'Obviously we were thrown out completely,' says Doyle, who figured later that it put him 35 minutes out in his calculations.

> I thought that I had plenty of time to get ready gradually. And all of a sudden I had to jump on my road bike and ride over there. I got into the stadium as the ride-off for third and fourth was more than halfway

Doyle's bike for 1988 world pursuit championships at Ghent where, for the first time, this starting gate was used. Notable features: the aerodynamic frame, disk wheels, seat pin (specially made for him), cowhorn handlebars and stem, and solid chain 'ring'

through. So that meant I was straight on for the final. And of course you're thrown into complete uproar.

Bennett was already there asking officials for a little more time, but the problem with following a set routine was that once it had been disrupted everything began to go wrong. Doyle had ridden to the track in his rubberised skinsuit, and because the outfit was very hot, tight-fitting and sweaty, his practice was to zip it to the top only just before he got to the line. And as bad luck would have it, when somebody helpfully tried to do it up for him, the zip broke.

'Now my parting words', says Doyle, 'as I left the cabin to dash across to the track were, don't forget my bag and make sure my crash hat is in it and a spare skinsuit. But they didn't. So I ended up needing to have the skinsuit taped up with wide adhesive tape and fastened together with safety pins.'

That was disconcerting enough for someone who is so punctilious about details. Worse, Doyle had to forgo his final warm-up; normally he would have spent 15 minutes just before the event working out on the rollers by the side of the track. As it was he started cold and without even time to compose himself. 'I was thinking to myself, I've been in the final four times so I've got the experience, while Piasecki has never been here before. But in body and in mind I just wasn't warmed up.'

Piasecki was ahead from the end of the first lap and built his lead to 2.68 sec after 11 laps. Doyle came back at him but it was now too late and Piasecki was home by 1.75 sec. The feeling of frustration and disappointment was hard to bear.

I have never felt so sure that a title was in my hands as I did that year. It was heart-breaking. I didn't explode. I'm very philosophical, though perhaps I was too philosophical for my own good at that time. I mean it happened, but it never should have happened. I'd arranged things, I'd planned things myself. I went along with that approach. Maybe there were too many people involved, but I felt that's what I needed, that taking such a serious approach was going to pay off. And if we hadn't made that mistake at the end it would have done. I would definitely have won a third world title.

De Wit went home at once, and says that for two weeks he was so depressed that he was practically in a coma. 'Tony and me are more like father and son. I was so certain that he was going to win, and then to be beaten by some stupidity – I was choked.' Meanwhile back at the hotel that evening, Doyle and his team held a gloomy and embarrassed post mortem. Much of the discussion hinged on which official schedule Bennett had been going by. The organisers publish a glossy programme well in advance which is not much more than a declaration of intent. This is then up-dated by a revised communiqué put out each evening to cover the next day's running order. Bennett was working from this. But the schedule is often altered yet again, perhaps to reflect the weather or unpredicted delays, or just to accomodate television. And this had been the case that day. But nobody had picked up the revised communiqué which had been issued during the midday interval. That was one slip-up. Whose? Maybe Bennett's. Maybe a collective responsibility. 'You can only be as efficient as the people around you,' he says.

More worrying, it emerged that one of the team had noticed that the events on the track no longer coincided with Doyle's schedule, but, although he had time to do so, had decided not to alert Bennett. It was still not clear why. It was a personal matter. 'At the end of it all, the team didn't function as one unit,' says Bennett. 'The personality side got to it, and it was my fault for not doing something about it earlier.'

He felt as badly as Doyle did about the breakdown, but could do no more than put it down to human error. He never thought that he had to go all out to make it up to Doyle, nor did Doyle ask him to. 'We had a great respect for one another, because he knew I wanted the best for him. I didn't gain financially from managing the team for him. It's just that he had done so much for me, helping me after the accident, which was quite traumatic, that I wanted to give the guy something back. I still feel that.' A year later, in the 1989 world championships at Lyons, he was once again helping Doyle at the trackside.

Doyle may not have let his anger off the leash at the time, but when I met him a few months later in the same city at the Ghent 6, he was still going over the same ground, naming – and blaming – names: 'Maybe I should get more irate. Maybe I should blow my top more when things go wrong.' Even when the summer came round he wasn't at all sure that he wanted to return to the world's. He decided he would wait and see how he felt.

As ever his confidence returned. Three weeks before the event, he says, his form was superb and he was feeling better than he had in 1988: 'I was screaming fit.' He put that down to his laid-back approach, and he planned an operation on similarly relaxed lines, with a small support group centred once more on Bennett, Cooke and de Wit.

Whether that method would have worked was never resolved. The day the world championships began Doyle developed an allergy which produced a reaction very like rheumatism in one of his legs. He rode and qualified in fourth place, but for the first time ever failed to get through to the semifinals; he was beaten by the American, Chris Huber, in the quarters. Instead the title went to another English rider, Colin Sturgess.

In the points race Sturgess was supposed to be riding for Doyle, but dropped out because his saddle was slipping, an explanation which left Bennett far from speechless. Doyle finished seventh. Later that year came the Munich crash, and, intent on making himself fit again for the six-day season, Doyle ignored the 1990 world championships in Japan. A year later, at Stuttgart, he was still not prepared for a return to the pursuit, riding only the points race, which he finished in 11th place.

That is the story so far: 12 years of world championships rewarded by two gold medals, four silver and one bronze, and marked by a good deal of injury and misfortune, by some straighforward failure through mis-calculation or lack of form, but, most of all, by perseverance. Doyle is unwilling to believe that he has contributed the final chapter. He admits that standards are particularly high at the moment with the emergence of the Frenchman, Francis Moreau, and the Soviet rider, Viatcheslav Ekimov, who have locked horns in a continuing struggle to set new world 5,000m records. But he would like to return to the world pursuit 'if everything fell into place'.

What drives him is the feeling that he has left unfinished business – 'that I haven't completely fulfilled my potential as a pusuiter; that I haven't done myself justice; and that the last twice I rode the world championships things happened which were out of my hands. That's why there's still something niggling away at the back of my mind saying, you ought to have another go. You don't plan bad luck, but it's the trials and tribulations that make success all the sweeter.'

Eddy Merckx, the Cannibal, and Patrick Sercu, the Phenomenon – the most successful riders ever in their different spheres – join the congratulations to Doyle who has just received his second world gold medal at Colorado Springs in 1986

171

A winter's tale 10

The season was winding down (though Doyle didn't realise quite how rapidly), and for its eleventh event the riders returned to Belgium for the Antwerp 6 in the north of the country close to the Dutch border. There have been Sixes on the same track at the Sportpaleis since 1934, and despite the fact that the interior has been modernised to accommodate ice shows and tennis tournaments, it's still a great barn of a place. One evening during the 1947 Six, in a period when all the spectator sports were booming, it fitted in a crowd of 28,000. but there wouldn't be too much pressure on space this week.

Compared with the previous German events it seemed low-key. After their rock and oompah music, the middle-aged easy listening of Karl Herberger en zijn Dansorkest proved less than inspiring, and there were no cafés, stalls and sideshows in the corridors around the hall. You came for the racing or nothing.

ANTWERP 6

Friday, 24 January

The 50th Antwerp 6 in its 58-year history, and so another Jubilee. My partner is Jelle Nijdam, the prologue specialist, Tour de France stage winner and member of the Buckler team. He is using the event as preparation for the road season which begins next week. He has ridden a couple of Sixes previously, but none since Paris four years ago, so he is a bit ring rusty.

The amateur Six, which started the evening programme, marked the debut of Axel Merckx, the 19-year-old son of the great Eddy. It was strange to see how nervous and apprehensive a great champion like Eddy could be when his own son was riding. He was worrying about Axel and shouting advice and encouragement to him from the trackside. You would have thought he had just ridden himself, the state he was in afterwards.

Saturday, 25 January

The Golden Night was pretty well wiped out by the weather. Thick fog kept the crowds away by the thousand. A disaster for the organisers. The night was marred, too, by a crash among the sprinters who had come on just after the big chase. They are amateurs who race twice an evening to give the pros a few minutes break. The one who came off worst in the crash was Curt Harnett, the Canadian Olympic prospect, who broke his collarbone.

It is always important to create the right atmosphere for the public and riders alike, and here there is a band playing live music, but oh what a choice of music. I kept waiting for David Jacobs or Angela Rippon to step forward and introduce 'Come Dancing'. It's certainly not the stuff to get the crowd going.

Sunday, 26 January

The fact that the track has been freezing cold hasn't helped to attract the spectators. They have had to keep hats, scarves and coats on, and I have been racing with extra under-jerseys plus arm-warmers and a neck-scarf.

Today the programme started early, at 12.45 pm, but at least we had an hour's break midway through the session when the amateurs hit the boards – quite literally in some cases.

I was pleased to win the big chase of the afternoon, particularly as Patrick Sercu was presenting the flowers. He commented on how well I was going, and that's generous coming from the Kaiser of the Sixes – 88 victories, and now race director at Moscow, Ghent, Bremen and Antwerp. Who says there's no life left when you hang up your wheels?

Nijdam was saying what good preparation the Six was. He was aiming for the classics, and in particular hoping to do well in the Tour of Flanders and the Paris–Roubaix.

Monday, 27 January

After an early finish yesterday, and a good night's sleep at Pierrot's house in Brussels, I went out with him for 90 minutes on a mountain bike to get some fresh air. Feeling really good and confident and raring to go and get on top of everything . . .

Which is as far as Tony Doyle's six-day diary went. Two-thirds of the way through the 50km madison, the second item in that evening's programme, Doyle went to change with Nijdam, something they had done scores of times on each of the last three days. They were midway along the home straight and halfway up the banking, with the field strung out in single file, which was the safest place to be. There should have been nothing to it. But this time Nijdam's wheel slid as he grasped for his partner's hand, and he brought Doyle crashing down with him in a heap.

Nijdam was unscathed. Doyle was in pain and left the trackside on a stretcher, but he was relieved to be told at the hospital that the X-ray showed no breakage. Pierrot was having an evening off, and his son, Stefan, had taken his place at the track. So it was he who drove back Doyle back to the house at one in the morning. Coming to the door, Pierrot, finding them in such good spirits, thought Doyle was trying to wind him up with this tale about a crash. When Doyle said he needed something to eat, Pierrot, normally the most solicitous of men, told him he knew where the food was kept and went back to bed.

Doyle crawled into the kitchen and then back to his bedroom. But he scarcely slept that night and felt even worse in the morning. Still he thought it was nothing serious, deep bruising or a muscle spasm, perhaps. And Pierrot, now persuaded that he had had a fall, suggested that they return early to the track to see how he felt after 15 minutes' warm-up. No, said Doyle, take me back to the hospital. And it was there that further X-rays and a CT scan revealed the truth: a broken pelvis.

Once back in Britain and out of traction, Doyle began pedalling away on a turbo trainer, and within a week he was back on his bike. He was taking, he said, 'an enforced rest after a demanding winter', and indeed there was no reason for long-term concern about the injury. All the same, there were three aspects of the crash that riled him.

Doyle felt that in so readily offering contracts to road race stars the promoters were showing little concern for the welfare of the six-day specialists who provided the skill and professionalism which kept the circuit going. The crash had come about through Nijdam's inexperience and consequent nervousness and uncertainty. He acknowledged Nijdam's road racing competence, 'but you don't put a horse like Desert Orchid into a race like the Derby and expect him to win it'.

He resented the fact that Nijdam had been more highly paid than himself for what was, in effect, a privileged week's fine tuning for the road season. And while the spill had not affected Nijdam's earning capacity, it had cost Doyle a contract to ride the final six-day of the season at Copenhagen and a six-hour meeting at San Sebastian on the following weekend.

More pointedly, he felt robbed of what might even be a last chance to ride and win with Clark, who was to have been his Copenhagen partner. He couldn't imagine anything stopping Clark and himself from taking the team record outright with a 20th victory together.

And there was one other thing he felt sensitive about. He didn't want, through no fault of his own, to get a reputation for being accident-prone.

Result: 1 Stan Tourné (Bel)/Jens Veggerby (Den), 281pts; 2 Pieters (Hol)/Freuler (Swi), 471pts, at one lap; 3 Bincoletto/ Baffi (It), 310pts, at 1 lap

At Copenhagen the outcome was just as Doyle had expected: victory for Clark, who had the good luck to be allotted another top partner.

Result: 1 Danny Clark (Australia)/Urs Freuler (Swi), 298pts; 2 De Wilde/Tourné (Bel), 247pts; 3 Veggerby (Den)/Bincoletto (It), 384pts, at 1 lap

Chapter 11

The right and wrong side of the tracks

Ideally, says Ron Webb, an Australian who has known Europe's indoor circuit as motor-paced rider, promoter and international track-builder, 'what you need for a six-day race is a big wooden bathtub, just 166–200m round: that's when you get the magical, electric atmosphere.' The spectators in the seating above look down as if into a whirlpool, and those in the track centre feel as though the current is whirling ceaselessly around their heads. Not every six-day has these wall-of-death tracks, but all depend on the theatrical qualities of intimacy, continuity, clamour and excitement, with the riders responding to the applause, and the audience to the racing.

My first sight of a Six was at Antwerp in the early 1960s. Until then I had only been to English open-air track meetings, notorious for their prolonged intervals, a lot of testing-one-two-three and not much lively information from the loudspeakers, and seemingly endless qualifying rounds of individual pursuit. Ghent was a revelation. Non-stop racing for pure entertainment. Trapeze artists swaying in the roof and a Tyrolean band blaring out polkas, marches and drinking songs from a dais. People in the track centre, which was as crowded as a cattle market, pouring champagne from ice-buckets and eating elaborate meals on trestle tables drawn right up to the side of the track. Prodigious amounts of Pilsner being put away by the more serious drinkers. And the air so blue with cigar smoke that you could scarcely see the other side of the track (I remember the Australian rider, Don Allan, telling me later that he used to cough black for a month after the event). Compared with the diffident sea-green amateur events at home, it all seemed brash and bright and thrillingly decadent.

The Six also had the self-contained life of a travelling fairground. The early 1960s saw the last efforts to keep the 144-year tradition alive, and although the track at Ghent was cleared in the morning between 5 am and 11 am, many of the old rituals were preserved. The racing was between three-man teams, and so there was always somebody slumbering in each trackside cabin. And on Sunday morning Mass was celebrated in the middle of the arena.

The music stands were taken down from the centre and an altar and carpet placed upon it. A waiter from one of the Sportpaleis restaurants, dressed for his daily work in tails, dapperly laid out the necessary vessels. A band dressed in pink, with circular brass horns – the Royal Hunting Club of Brasschaat – formed up at one side. And as a pale, religious light slanted in from the high windows, a flat-hatted Belgian wandered in, chewing an unlighted cigar, not quite certain whether or not he was in church. As a compromise he put out his cigar but left his hat on.

With a congregation of townspeople already gathering, the cyclists began to file into the front row, except for two who were enlisted by l'abbé Van Dijck to serve as altar boys. The choir brought in from the church of the Holy Family sang to their intensely intellectual conductor. And those who were there on business, the mechanics and photographers, simply went about it. Twenty minutes later, with the service at an end, the riders got back to their daily round, sitting upright as they pedalled with one foot and steered with the other, chatting among themselves. The attendants shepherded the congregation out, making sure that none of them stayed on as a spectator.

At Ghent the track was the focus of all activity – eating, drinking, music and variety entertainment – and that's still the pattern at Belgian six-day races. In German Sixes and at Zurich the action tends to overflow into all the surrounding corridors and foyers. Their aim is to lay on an animated *Bierfest* both for those who take a serious interest in cycle racing and those who just like the atmosphere of a noisy party where there's plenty going on. Webb warns you never to confuse the attendance figure with payments at the box office. 'When Sixes say they had 60,000 spectators over the week, it often means that they gave out 30,000 complimentaries. It doesn't matter whether they pay as long as they come in and eat the sausages and drink the beer.'

At Dortmund, Munich, Antwerp and Zurich, giant lorry doors open at the end of the track so that fresh supplies can be driven in. And if the last attempt to revive the Hanover 6 in 1979–81 was sadly short-lived, this was not the fault of the local trenchermen who in the course of any evening got through 2,000 bratwurst, 3,500 bockwurst, 1,500 meatballs, 3,000 open fish sandwiches, one whole roasted ox, 13,000 litres of beer, 12,000 glasses of schnapps, and 4,500 colas. Naturally, they would have eaten before they came out.

At the old Skol 6s at Wembley, which provide the most marked contrast, the crowds were largely made up of club parties of bikies intent on watching every minute of the action. They passed round the hat to put up extra primes for the riders, filled in their programmes, cheered everything that moved and only left their seats at the interval. In Germany even the fans are inclined to pick and choose what they watch, and a few of the casuals come into the velodrome only for the floor show. At Stuttgart recently, where the show consisted of acrobatic dancers and a team of English trampolinists, the counter-attractions on two tiers of galleries outside included biergartens, wine bars, restaurants, ox roast, shops and exhibitions, and the 'Six-Days Nightclub' with go-go girls and two-hourly strip show (closed on Family Day).

Sixes come and go. There were 12 in Europe during the 1991–92 season compared with 17 a decade before. Berlin, Münster, Paris, Madrid, Brussels and Milan have dropped from the circuit; so have Rotterdam and Maastricht, leaving the Netherlands, the home of Peter Post and René Pijnen, with none at all. Perhaps this is temporary; it's hard to believe that a sport like cycle racing, which maintains a huge following on the Continent, will lose interest in its winter spectacular. Antwerp dropped out for four years while the hall was remodelled to suit indoor tennis, but returned in 1987. Vienna hopes to build its current three-day event into a Six. And just before Christmas 1991, as much to its own surprise as everyone else's, Moscow found itself plugged into the six-day circuit for the very first time.

It would be stretching the truth to say that the Moscow event was an instant success with the public, but the prospects of a repeat will presumably depend upon whether its two German sponsors, Beck's Beer and the electronics firm Siemens, decide that it gave them the commercial exposure they hoped for. The tepid public response was hardly surprising in a country which was going through one political revolution after another. With food running out in the shops and money losing value, people were not in a mood to be diverted by a cycle race imported at a cost of £525,000 – not even if two Soviet cyclists led it from start to finish. But mistiming wasn't the only problem.

The promoter, Frank Minder, who has the advertising and sponsorship franchise for the Bremen 6, said he resolved to bring the event to Moscow on first seeing the Krylatskoye Olympic velodrome. It is a splendid track, but its dizzy bankings proved too slippery to allow madison chases every night, and so this became a six-day race without its one essential feature. The track was also huge – three laps to the kilometre – so that the building which housed it, while again impressive, was far too big to generate warmth and excitement. And beside being remote from the centre, it was not on the Metro, the city's one reliable means of public transport.

Most other problems were down to local disorganisation. Minder had billed the event as: 'Six nights with Sport. Show. Music. Original German beer. International food.' And perhaps it was just as well that his bills were next to invisible around Moscow. Where was the international food? Only in the track centre, disguised as pizza from the Pizza Hut stall. And, like the beer and *Sekt*, it was available only for dollars and deutschmarks, which the Muscovites didn't have. Sausages and other German foods, meant to be sold for roubles in the stands, simply hadn't turned up. According to a journalist from *Sport-Express*, spectators were incensed to see Germans, who had been thrown back from the gates of their city half a century before, publicly tucking into food which they couldn't afford.

The riders also felt let down. They had been promised good hotel rooms, but when they arrived in a party two hours late from Frankfurt, they were shown to shabby riders' quarters at the track. Even the best of these were patrolled by cockroaches, and the worst were too filthy to use. After talk of a riders' strike they were moved first to an army officers' hostel and next day to a tourist hotel. The show went on. As usual the promoter had won them round.

It's nothing rare for those who pay the rider in pro cycling – sponsor, manager, organiser or promoter – to call the tune. When Félix Lévitan was running the Tour de France in the 1980s, he often did so in bland defiance of the rules of the world governing body, the Union Cycliste Internationale (UCI). But no branch of the sport is quite so promoter-led as six-day cycling. The promoters select the riders, divide them into teams of their own choice, determine their rates of pay and conditions of employment. In Germany, for instance, they pay the riders a day-rate. But it covers only five days, not six, since they reckon that although the riders race six nights they only race five days. The benefit of this dubious argument, as usual goes to the promoters.

Benevolent or not, they are dictators. In road racing, if a rider falls out with his employers he can transfer to others and go on riding in the same events. In six-day racing the promoter is employer and event organiser in one, and if the rider falls out with him, or earns a general reputation for awkwardness among the members of the promoters' cartel, the International Union of Velodromes (UIV), he has nowhere else to turn. 'If you have a blazing row with one promoter,' says Doyle, 'you can get a bad reputation which can spread like wildfire.'

The question arises whether the promoters, having picked the teams to produce a certain kind of race, then put pressure on the the riders to produce a good box-office result. The suspicion that they do is fanned by the number of wins by local riders, very often at the eleventh hour (or even after the clock has struck midnight, if you think back to Grenoble 1991, when the Doyle-Roche victory was overturned in favour of the French team). Doyle admits there have been times when he has been told that the promoter would like a certain team to win, 'but very, very rarely'. He deeply resents the use of the word 'circus' to describe the sport, as though it were more an exhibition than an open contest: a kind of Harlem Globetrotters on wheels. And he contends that his record with Danny Clark is proof enough that they ride to win.

The unfair pressure, he suggests, is more likely to come from riders who, while not paired in the Six, compete together for the same sponsor during the road season. At Munich in 1991, for instance, Doyle and Clark were riding together. On the track, too, were De Wilde and Kappes, the eventual winners, who were both contracted to the Sigma team but about to join Telecom. Another man, Stumpf, was in the same situation. Woods, Durich and Hass were already with Telecom.

Now they were all going to be riding alongside De Wilde in the summer, so initially they were going to be looking after their own interests. They might have been be teamed up as rivals to them, but while they wouldn't be doing anything to help De Wilde and Kappes, they wouldn't be doing anything against them. A little hesitation when chasing in the madison. That sort of thing. There's bound to be a certain amount of favouritism and friction. And anyway riders ride for the national flag. They'll rally round one of their own even if there's no money changing hands and no pressure from the sponsors.

Doyle, who has never belonged to a year-round trade team with strong Continental connections in the sport, organises his own six-day contracts – either directly with the promoters or through Jan Dirksen, an old sprint rival of Reg Harris, who acts as manager for most of the riders on a standard 10 per cent commission. Recently there has been some talk of setting up a 'union' to give the riders more muscle in their dealings with promoters. But although only at the discussion stage so far, it doesn't appear to be what the TUC would recognise as a union, open to all, more a senior riders' pressure group. So far the proposal is for Heinz Betz, a former six-day man who looks after many German riders' interests, to act for, say, 14 of the established regulars. He would negotiate minimum contracts for them at all the Sixes, and these would include hotel accommodation for them and their personnel. But on the face of it this would be no more than an extension of the agent system, with the Blue Train negotiating from combined strength instead of individually. It would do little to help newcomers from being exploited; in fact it would probably make their position worse.

When Doyle turned pro his £150 a month from KP showed poorly against the £250 he had been getting as a salesman at Selfridges. And although £85 a day at the Skol 6 was comparative riches, even that was hard-earned for a young man with a rainbow jersey on his back. There is still a wide gulf in the fees paid to the stars and those to the supporting cast. Few people in competitive jobs are keen to show you their payslips, and in the cut-throat world of the Sixes the reluctance is that much more acute.

179

On the basis of informed conjecture, a top rider like Danny Clark will probably earn on average £10–12,000 for a Six, which means around £100,000 a year, excluding sponsorship. But even at the top there are wide variations between the perceived value of different riders and the rates paid at different events; and at the bottom those with modest records have to be content with as little as £2,000–2,500 for six days' of risk and fatigue.

Six-day riders are resigned to the fact that road racing has by far the higher profile and that in recent years its rewards have soared while theirs have risen only gradually. Nobody on the boards can boast a deal within light years of Greg LeMond's three-year, £3.7 million contract with the French Z team. But what does rile them is that the roadmen are just as disproportionately paid when they invade the winter tracks. World champions like Rudy Dhaenens or Gianni Bugno command around £20,000–25,000 for the week's work.

Even back in 1977, Didi Thurau, Germany's 22-year-old 'Blond Angel', having just won five stages in the Tour de France, worn the yellow jersey for a fortnight and finished fifth, was getting £3,000 a day to ride in six-days at home, and £500 for autograph-signing sessions in the big stores. Always the pragmatist, Doyle accepts that these riders add to the interest and prestige of the event: 'Go back a hundred years, and the track was the glory side of the sport, now it's the road. Because they're just making the odd appearance, they get the media attention.' Often, though, it's the regulars who have to pay for it. The roadmen's unease in the fast-flowing traffic on the track makes everyone else nervous and increases the risk of accident, as Doyle experienced to his cost at Antwerp in 1992 when Jelle Nijdam slid into him and brought his season to a premature end.

In addition to the basic appearance money in the contract, there are prizes to be gained during any Six for winning the sprint series or the chase, or setting lap records, or simply for being first across the line after so many laps. Usually the most valuable of these prizes are the gleaming new saloons displayed on a dais or a revolving turntable in the track centre (in the 1950s and 1960s the Swiss sprinter, Fritz Pfenninger, won a record 43). Originally the cars were meant for the winner's own use. But after a manufacturer discovered that one winner had sold his prize to a showroom for less than cost-price – so that both were losing on the deal – cash was substituted for the car itself; and that was often split between a combine of riders who had carved up the competition between them.

It's extremely hard to put a value on the convertible prizes on offer at a Six. One man who has been a promoter reckons that it is around £1,000 – enough, anyway, to cover the riders' travel and personnel expenses. Doyle says this is untrue.

Prizes are just a front for the public. They think how fortunate you are to have won a new BMW 8-series – and I must have won, I don't know, 20 cars – but the only time you drive one is when you sit in it for your lap of honour. You're not even given the keys or a scale model souvenir. Riders used to win them, but it's not the case now. As for primes donated by the public, they were unique to Wembley. In my time, anyway. Often you're presented with a record player on the finish line. At least that's what it looks like. But nine times out of ten you do your lap of honour with an empty box, and more often than not what was in it is retained by the promoters. Occasionally there will be money or prizes donated by sponsors, and they'll be split up among the riders, but they don't come to much. Over a winter you will get cups, trophies, maybe a radio cassette, a walkman, champagne, little bits and pieces, and you get to keep them. But the big things are siphoned off.

What the rider receives is his contract, a year-long deal with a team or sponsor, and any prize money he wins in road races. The world championships cost you money. When I last won a world title in 1986 the prize was £650, which is a fraction of what I had spent on preparation. There is money to be earned off the bike, but you'll have much more opportunity for doing that if you are Belgian or Dutch than if you're British or Australian, because the sport has a far higher profile in their countries – promoting casual wear, formal wear, sunglasses, after-shave, bikes, crash-helmets, massage cream and so on. You may get a column in a daily newspaper, or work on radio and TV, and be paid to open shops and fêtes. If I do any of that it's normally for free. What passport you hold is going to affect your bank balance.

As for expenses, there's a manager's fee, which is 10–15 per cent of earnings; then a withholding tax from the country where the rider competes, which will be 15–40 per cent; and in most countries, the cycling federation will take a cut of, say, 2 per cent. There is the charge for his own and his helpers' use of the riders' kitchen, which comes to £200–250, and the variable cost of travel and hotels. Then there are the wages to the personnel. Although they work for more than one rider, each rider will pay the soigneur £3–400 for his services at an event, the mechanic £2–300, and the runner £150.

The prudent rider also pays medical insurance – which in Doyle's case comes to about £1,500 a year:

It's up to the rider himself, but I learned my lesson from Danny, who had a serious accident back in 1983. On the second night at Frankfurt he came down and broke his hip, and at the time he didn't have any insurance. After losing best part of a season he knows it's important. It's a high-risk sport and you never know what's around the banking.

181

Doyle's soigneur is Pierrot de Wit, whose essential role has already been explained. Up to Munich 1989, his six-day mechanic was Bob Arnold, who then took a job at the Staines Bicyclecraft shop but still looks after Doyle's bikes in Britain. Now Doyle's mechanic is the Belgian, Hector Zelk, who is also employed by Stan Tourné. At the start of each winter season, Doyle gives Zech two bikes and eight pairs of wheels and spares, and his job is not just to maintain them but transport them from one event to the next. It is typical of Doyle, though, that he always keeps a spare bike and wheels at home, crated up and ready to be flown out in case of emergency. Also on the strength is his runner and general gofer, a bus-driver who lives near Lyons and is known throughout the camp as Bon-Bon.

Where once the Six was a world apart, apparently subject only to market forces, it has now been brought closer to the cycling mainstream. One aspect of this is the introduction over the past three seasons of regular dope tests. Urine samples are taken twice – on the third and on the final days – from one rider in each of the top three teams and from two riders picked at random: a higher percentage of the field than in most road races. In that time only one rider, Urs Freuler, has been suspended. Amphetamine was detected by a control at the Munich 6 in 1990, and then a further charge of testosterone use was made at a German criterium in 1991. Etienne De Wilde, too, gave a positive result for anabolic steroid at Antwerp in 1987, when testing was more the exception than the rule, but was not suspended. Both riders have disputed these findings in the courts.

Given the arduous, repetitive nature of the sport (and assuming that all the tests have been above board), this might seem a surprisingly low proportion of positive tests. But it doesn't surprise Doyle, who believes that the high proportion of six-day riders who go on competing well into their 30s, and are alive to tell the tale in their 80s, speaks for itself.

If dope controls, like the award of FICP points, bring the Sixes more into line with the summer sport, so does the gradual improvement in the riders' living conditions. If any mourned the passing of the Berlin 6 after 80 years – Doyle and Clark conducting the last rites with their 1988 victory – they shed few tears for the Deutschland Halle itself, where the event was latterly held. The track came down with the Berlin Wall, though in this case the pressures were commercial; it was taking up space needed for conferences, exhibitions and concerts. On the final night there was scarcely a damp eye among the riders who had spent their nights in its atrocious quarters. Right to the end they had been obliged to sleep on site, as though they might still be called out on the track at any moment to entertain the ghostly spectators of the 1920s.

By this time Doyle and Clark had graduated from their former dormitory to a bedroom of their own. Well, in a manner of speaking. It was an underground cabin into which it was only just possible to fit two beds and mattresses, without pillows, sheets or duvets, which they had to carry with them from place to place like travelling people. In addition there was one small table and two chairs, though not enough space for two people to sit at that table. No wardrobe was provided, so they had to hang their clothes from the heating pipes which ran across the ceiling. The stifling temperature and the sound of pumping water made it difficult to sleep. To these discomforts were added the smells from the kitchen just along the corridor. Doyle and Clark might be aboard the Blue Train by now, but their couchettes were distinctly third-class.

At Dortmund the velodrome was part of a hotel complex, and the riders enjoyed the luxury of staying in the same rooms as the guests. But that was the exception. At most tracks they were required to live in, and their quarters varied only by degrees. And at Zurich in mid-winter they had, until recently, to sleep in caravans in the car park. Zurich was the only place which made them yearn for the fug of their Berlin bunkers. Zurich was the pits.

It wasn't just the sleeping arrangements, it was the working hours, and these are still the same. The race is kept going until the trams start the next day. This may be justified at the weekend, and particularly on the closing Saturday, when the racing starts at 3.30 in the afternoon and there is still a crowd of 13–14,000 spectators at five on the Sunday morning. But earlier in the week the crowd will have thinned to a few hundred drunks by the early hours; people who have to work next day can't afford to see the whole programme through.

So when you finished each night, by the time you'd showered and changed, had a light massage and something to eat it would be six or seven before you were going to bed. So you'd go out across the yard to your caravan. Zurich at dawn in December, you can imagine how cold it was. The caravans were heated by gas, and I remember numerous times going back to find that the cylinder had run out. So you'd get into your sleeping bag and try to keep warm by putting on your racing cap and gloves and socks. And then you'd attempt to go to sleep. But by now daylight had broken, the rush hour traffic was building up, and everyone was going to work. Not exactly the lap of luxury.

Many of the older promoters hankered after a golden age before their time when riders knew their place, pedalled through the night and were grateful for a bench to curl up on. Even when Doyle began his career, some of them kept up the pretence that racing was continuous. One man from each team had to remain on the track at all times, including the interval when the show was put on. And although the hall was in darkness except for the spotlights on the performers, and everyone was watching their act, the riders had to

183

circle above the blue line, which meant keeping up 20mph for the sake of balance. Even when they couldn't be seen they weren't allowed to switch off and relax.

Joseph Voegli, promoter of the Zurich 6 (and also of the Tour of Switzerland), is one of the last of the old martinets. A hard man, proud of the iron regime of his Six. Riders, by way of illustration, like to point to the fact that he employs his own brother as a cleaner at the track. Until recently he would not let riders leave the building and the compound for the duration of the event, and when one of them, Albert Fritz, pleaded that he needed a haircut, Voegli brought a barber in to him.

In 1990, at the meeting before the first night's racing, he issued an ultimatum that no full crash hats, no shorts with coloured panels and no fluorescent socks must be worn. Why? Because this was Zurich, and there were standards to keep up.

When he finished I had a word with him. Unfortunately in the Munich accident, I said, I had a very serious head injury, and since these things are cumulative, I have to a wear a very strong, full crash hat. He said, "For you Tony, I'll make a special exception." As the Six wore on he relented. After all, if you ride for Histor or Panasonic, your shorts have a blue or red panel on them. You're not given special shorts for Zurich. Hardly anyone had plain black shorts, and nobody uses plain black socks any more. All the same, that's the tradition, and that's what he would have liked.

Another concession from Voegli is that riders may now stay in hotels – at their own expense. And that has become the general rule. At Cologne a number of the riders still stay in; the conditions are tolerable, it saves them cash and bother, and since they work the same hours as nightclub waiters, they don't always find it easy to get to their hotels. At Stuttgart, for instance, the Schleyerhalle is next to the football stadium, and the hotel which serves them both – a basic kind of *pension* used by sportsmen who come to train there – is a kilometre away. 'I can remember trudging there in the early morning through six inches of snow.'

It's the freedom to get away from the stadium that's important. 'In a hotel they lose track of you, though even then you don't have any contact with the outside world except by phoning home. There could be a bubonic plague raging and you wouldn't know.' Some years ago, before the old monastic order was relaxed, Doyle described his way of life to me as 'a self-chosen penance ... You stay at the track and eat and sleep underground, At Munich ten days ago the first fresh air I smelt was in the taxi on the way to the station.'

The move had to be made, if only to make the sport acceptable to the road race stars whom the promoters wanted to attract. If the six-day regulars had become institutionalised, accepting the lodgings as part of the job, the roadmen were used to 3-star comfort, at least, and a change of scenery.

In other respects there have been few improvements, and the daily workplace remains pretty squalid. Visiting Doyle in his massage room at Ghent you had to walk across a grilled floor which resembled nothing so much as one of the landings at Pentonville. The comparison hasn't escaped Doyle, who once said to a reporter: 'Asking me which track I prefer is like asking Buster Edwards to name his favourite prison.'

The trackside cabins, too, are little different from what they were 70 years ago: a terraced shanty town of plywood huts, each just big enough to hold a bed, a shelf for drinks, snacks and embrocations, and a slop bucket. A curtain, which looks like an overdue discard from someone's front room, provides scant privacy. What used to be the rider's home, in the days when he did two hours on and two hours off the track, is now his retreat in those short intervals between races. It's where he changes his shirt and undershirt (the latter often 15 times a night), gets a light massage, and performs his natural functions in the bucket which the runner will carry back under the track to empty. Returning to one of his favourite similes, Doyle says, 'It may be practical, but imagine Boris Becker at Wimbledon, and after the third set him going into a wooden closet at the edge of the court, hauling a flimsy bit of curtain across, and sitting down and doing his business with all the eyes of the spectators and television on him.'

The private dining room at the track, always referred to as the riders' kitchen, is no more inviting, either, than the average workshop canteen. But at least the food is of a kind the riders need. Since Doyle has been in the sport it has been run at most Sixes by a German couple, the Dampkes, living the same nomadic life as their customers (the rider pays for himself and for his personnel). Now that she has been widowed, Helen Dampke carries on the tradition.

The riders are extremely fussy about their food which, however monotonous, must be substantial without being heavy, and above all must be clean. In the close, unhygienic conditions of the track centre, intestinal upsets quickly spread. They are as great an occupational hazard as the sores, chafing and open wounds which result from prolonged contact with the saddle. This is common to all long-distance cyclists, but the strain is intensified for trackmen by the G-forces which are exerted as they come into and out of the banking, especially when they are riding behind the dernys.

A year after he began his career in six-day races, Doyle helpfully passed on what he had learnt to the readers of *Cycling* magazine:

I use a baby cream from Mothercare called Natusan; some use Savlon. You need fresh shorts each night and they should be treated with chamois fat an hour to an hour-and-a-half before wearing. Fresh fat is applied before the derny racing and before the last madison. Afterwards you clean down with soap and water and apply eau de Cologne. You have to look after the chamois.

Track, trackside cabin, riders' kitchen, massage cabin, bedroom: these mark the periphery of the small world which the riders occupy for all but a week. During that time almost every hour of every day is monopolised by riding, sleeping, eating and preparing. Characteristically Doyle's programme goes like this: Get up at midday. Breakfast on ham, cheese and rolls, muesli and coffee; maybe an omelette as well. If there is afternoon racing, go straight on to the main massage. If not, read and relax, make phone calls, until the main meal of the day at five (the standard two hours before starting racing or training). The runner will already have ordered this and laid the table in the riders' kitchen. It will probably consist of minestrone soup, then salad followed by chicken with rice or with pasta and vegetables. Round off with fresh fruit and yoghurt and coffee. Finish the meal by 5.30. Have the main massage if it hasn't been done before. Or if there has been an afternoon session, go back to hotel bedroom or quarters to kip for 60–75 minutes. Back to the track.

During the evening many riders nibble away at energy bars, cut-up apples left in water or sweet biscuits with honey whenever they return to the trackside cabin. But Doyle doesn't eat at all, however late the finish. He prefers to take his food in liquid form with a carbohydrate polymer drink. 'One problem is to keep food down. You don't want to feel too bloated when you are whacking around that banking. Often when riders come for the first time they go through the same effects as sea-sickness. They are not used to the weaving in and out and the G-force, and they have to leave the track to be sick.'

In the early hours, after the racing is over, they head for a cold supper which the kitchen staff have left out for the riders: salad, chicken, omelette and cheese, honey sandwiches, fruit and yoghurt. And so to bed.

Played out in a strange, twilight world, it is a hard, repetitive life which few would envy. Even ambitious young racing cyclists – partly because they have never watched a six-day race unfold in their own country, as Doyle did with growing fascination as a boy – are far more likely to be drawn towards the richer, more varied and more glamorous road game. But Doyle, apart from possessing the gifts, seems to have the temperament for it: 'Part of the battle is to learn to accept conditions. If you constantly rebel you get so worked up tht you're unable to go through with it. The sooner you accept the situation the easier it is to cope.'

That may sound submissive, but it's more complicated than that. Doyle has a remarkable capacity for cutting himself off from disappointment, unpleasantness and just minor irritations. He has taken a lot of hard knocks, some literal and some even more hurtful because they were on a personal level. But although he can nurse a grievance over many years, he gets to a stage where he can poke fun at it. His long-standing disagreement with Jim Hendry, for instance. He wonders aloud whether he shouldn't have blown his top at the time, but you know he doesn't really mean it. That's not his style. His one obvious safety valve is his sarcasm. But the habit-forming pleasures of bitterness are something he seems to have well under control; he has given them up in the way that others give up smoking or taking sugar in their tea. It's an impediment to getting what he really wants.

Almost alone among his fellow riders, he is a compulsive reader. He brings a small batch of paperbacks to each Six and reckons to get through two or three of them. Adventure novels mostly – Alistair McLean, Len Deighton, Desmond Bagley. But at Ghent the other year he was reading Melvyn Bragg's biography of Richard Burton, and at Moscow in 1991 he was just getting into a book about his recently deceased sponsor, Robert Maxwell. With bicycles whirring round his head and the synthesised din of Ludwigs Disco in his ears, he will sit on a chair outside his cabin concentrating on a book and apparently lost to everything else. 'It's books and your walkman that keep you sane.'

Yet you know that once the moment comes to get back on the track, he will be in there competing. And if he isn't thoroughly enjoying himself, he is fooling an awful lot of people, including himself. I'm convinced that isn't the case. He is the perpetual optimist. The next race, the next championship, the next season is always going to be better than the last. A few days after he had broken his pelvis at Antwerp in 1992 he was back on his turbo-trainer, talking confidently of a quick recovery and the benefit of an unscheduled spell of rest.

He enjoys both his senior position in the sport and the camaraderie of the kitchen. With some basic German and fluent riders' French, he can join easily in the small talk. And if the walls of the prison house begin to close, he always knows that in a few days he will pay a flying visit home, or that Anne and the family will be coming out to see him. That if events run true to form, he and Anne will take a short December break in Miami, and at the end of five months, which always pass more quickly than he expected, they will be skiing near Grenoble, where he can clear the accumulated winter smoke from his lungs. At 34 he gives himself another five or six years on the winter tracks. And why not? After the first 12 years he is just as happy and even more successful in his work.

Tony Doyle: personal record

Born Hampton Court, Middlesex, 19 May 1958

1972   Joined Clarence Wheelers
1975   British junior 3km pursuit bronze medal
1976   Winner, Peak Forest race, Charles Viner Memorial (Peter Buckley series)
Winner, Montreal amateur six-day race (with Steve Heffernan and Ian Banbury)
1977   Winner, Manchester–Rhyl two-day race
British 4km pursuit champion and amateur madison champion (with Glen Mitchell)
1978   Winner, Ras de Cymru
British 4km pursuit champion
Commonwealth Games, Edmonton, individual and team pursuit bronze medals
1979   British 4km pursuit champion, amateur points champion and amateur madison champion (with Glen Mitchell)
1980   Married Anne D'Rozario, 9 February
Quarter-finalist in Olympic team pursuit, Moscow
Took out professional licence, 4 August
World 5km pursuit champion (Besançon)
British 5km pursuit champion
1980/81★   Rode first professional six-day race, Skol 6 at Wembley, with Udo Hempel (Ger); finished 8th.
Other six-day races with places in top eight: Berlin, 7th (Horst Schutz, Ger); Grenoble, 6th (Hans Hindelang, Ger); Rotterdam, 6th (Maurice Burton, GB); Copenhagen, 5th (Burton); Hanover, 8th (Stan Tourné, Bel)
European omnium championships (Zurich), silver medal
1981   British 5km pursuit champion (with British record)
1981/82   Six-day races: Grenoble, 7th (Serge Beucherie, Fr); Herning, 5th (Hans Hindelang, Ger); Copenhagen, 7th (Jorge Marcussen, Den)
1982   British 5km pursuit champion (with British outdoor 5km record)
World 5km pursuit (Leicester), 4th
1982/83   Six-day races: Copenhagen, 5th (Stan Tourné, Bel)
European omnium championships (Herning), bronze medal
1983   Sealink International: won Birmingham–Sheffield stage; finished second overall
World 5km pursuit, 4th; world points race, 5th (both events at Zurich)
1983/84   Six-day races: Berlin, **1st** (Danny Clark, Australia); Dortmund, **1st** (Clark); Munich, 4th (Gary Wiggins, Australia); Zurich, 4th (Wiggins); Herning, 4th (Wiggins); Bremen, 2nd (Wiggins); Rotterdam, 7th (Clark); Copenhagen, 4th (Wiggins); Milan, 4th (Wiggins)
1984   Sealink International: 1st prologue, Skelmersdale; finished second overall
World 5km pursuit (Barcelona), silver medal
1984/85   Six-day races: Dortmund, 8th (Rolf Hofeditz, Ger); Munich, 4th (Gary Wiggins, Australia); Ghent, 3rd (Danny Clark, Australia); Zurich, 3rd (Wiggins); Maastricht, 4th (Wiggins); Bremen, 1st (Wiggins); Rotterdam, 6th (Wiggins)
European madison championships (Zurich), gold medal with Gary Wiggins (Australia)
1985   Sealink International: won Buxton and Kirby stages; finished fifth overall
World 5km pursuit (Bassano), silver medal
1985/86   Six-day races: Berlin, 3rd (Joachim Schlaphof, Ger); Dortmund, 3rd (Stephen Roche, Ire); Munich, 3rd (Gary Wiggins, Australia); Paris, 2nd (Roche); Ghent, 2nd (Michel

Vaarten, Bel); Zurich, 5th (Wiggins); Maastricht, 1st (Danny Clark, Australia); Bremen, 6th (Wiggins); Stuttgart, 3rd (Clark); Copenhagen, 1st (Clark)

European madison championships (Copenhagen), silver medal with Gary Wiggins (Australia)

1986   British 5km pursuit champion

World 5km pursuit champion (Colorado Springs); world's fastest outdoor 5km pursuit (still stands)

Launceston 6, 1st (Clark)

1986/87   Six-day races: Berlin, 1st (Danny Clark, Australia); Dortmund, 1st (Clark); Grenoble, 1st (Francisco Moser, It); Munich, 5th (Gary Wiggins, Australia); Paris, 2nd (Charly Mottet, Fr); Ghent, 1st (Clark); Zurich, 4th (Jorge Muller, Swi); Maastricht, 2nd (Clark); Bremen, 7th (Laurent Fignon, Fr); Stuttgart, 2nd (Moser); Rotterdam, 6th (Fignon); Copenhagen, 1st (Clark)

European madison championships (Copenhagen), silver medal with Gary Wiggins (Australia)

1987   Bassano del Grappa 6 (outdoor), 1st (Moreno Argentin, It/Roman Hermann, Liechtenstein)

National 5km pursuit champion

World 5km pursuit, bronze medal; world points race, silver medal (both events, Vienna)

1987/88   Six-day races: Antwerp, 3rd (Eric Vanderaerden, Bel); Berlin, 2nd (Danny Clark, Australia); Dortmund, 3rd (Roland Gunther, Ger); Grenoble, 2nd (Etienne De Wilde, Bel); Munich, 2nd (Clark); Zurich, 2nd (Hermann); Maastricht, 1st (Clark); Cologne, 2nd (Hans-Henrik Oersted, Den); Bremen, 1st (Clark); Rotterdam, 1st (Clark); Stuttgart, 2nd (Clark); Copenhagen, 2nd (Clark); Paris, 1st (Clark)

1988   Awarded MBE

National 5km pursuit champion, with British record

World 5km pursuit (Ghent), silver medal

1988/89   Six-day races: Antwerp, 3rd (Adriano Baffi, It); Münster, 1st (Danny Clark, Australia); Berlin, 1st (Clark); Dortmund, 1st (Clark); Grenoble, 5th (Greg LeMond); Munich, 1st (Clark); Ghent, 3rd (Clark); Zurich, 5th (Clark); Cologne, 1st (Clark); Bremen, 5th (Dietrich Thurau, Ger); Stuttgart, 7th (Bernt Grone, Ger); Copenhagen, 2nd (Michael Marcussen, Den)

European omnium championships, gold medal; European madison championships, gold medal (with Danny Clark, Australia) (both events, Copenhagen)

1989   Milk Race: won stage 8, Preston–Harrogate

World 5km pursuit, lost in q-f, finishing fifth; world points race, 7th (both events, Lyons)

1989/90   Six-day races: Paris, 5th (Pascal Lino, Fr); Dortmund, 2nd (Torsten Rellensman, Ger); Grenoble, 5th (Jean-Claude Colotti, Fr); Munich, injured in crash on fourth night and missed rest of season

European madison championships (Ghent); gold medal with Danny Clark (Australia)

1990/91   Six-day races: Dortmund, 5th (Torsten Rellensman, Ger); Grenoble, 4th (Rik Van Slycke, Bel); Munich, 1st (Danny Clark, Australia); Bordeaux, 2nd (Pascal Lino, Fr); Ghent, 4th (Stan Tourné, Bel); Zurich, 5th (Bruno Holenweger, Swi); Stuttgart, 4th (Urs Freuler, Swi); Antwerp, 5th (Eric Vanderaerden, Bel); Copenhagen, 6th (Michael Marcussen, Den)

1991   Won Newport Nocturne and Bryn Bach Classic

1991/92   Six-day races: Dortmund, 7th (Tourné, Bel); Grenoble, 2nd (Stephen Roche, Ire); Munich, 3rd (Danny Clark, Australia); Ghent, 1st (Etienne De Wilde, Belg); Zurich, 6th (Tourné); Moscow, 3rd (Clark); Cologne, 5th (Dean Woods, Australia); Bremen, 3rd (Clark); Stuttgart, 6th (Woods); Antwerp: retired after breaking his pelvis in a fall on the fourth night, so also missing the final Six at Copenhagen

winter season

Glossary

à l'américaine: term in general use on the Continent, since French is the official language of cycle racing, for what is known in Britain as a *madison* and in the USA as a team race.

Balustrade sprints: sprints from a standing start in which the riders line up along the top of the straight, and for balance hold on to the balustrade with their right hands.

Blue Train: the inner circle of 16–20 recognised six-day riders who regularly contribute nearly half the field at each event. The numbers are then made up, usually to 32, by riders recruited on a casual basis and varying from venue to venue. These will include novice six-day riders searching for experience and recognition; popular home-town and home-country riders who rarely get contracts elsewhere; and stars from other sections of the sport, in particular road racing, who are expensively hired by promoters for their publicity value.

Cabins: riders' temporary quarters. Trackside cabins are rows of simple plywood/hardboard boxes furnished with a bed for rest and light massage and a curtain for privacy; usually they occupy one of the ends of the track centre. Massage cabins are rooms elsewhere in the stadium used for that purpose, and sometimes – though less frequently nowadays – doubling as bedrooms.

Chase: the *madison* relay, in particular any spell of it when riders are going flat out to improve or defend their positions in the race.

Criterium: road race over so many laps of a small, enclosed circuit, and usually passing through built-up areas. There is no standard length to the race, but as the object is to provide spectators with near-continuous entertainment, the laps are rarely more than 4–6km long.

Derny: a light motor-powered cycle which can be pedal-assisted by the driver using a high gearing connected to the pedals. It was developed for motor-paced racing on indoor tracks too small and tight to suit the special 2,200cc 'big motors' used outdoors. The derny's other advantage is that it can be followed by riders using their normal track bikes, not the modified machines with small front wheels and reversed forks needed for riding behind the big motors. This also makes it ideal for sustained speed training, indoors or out.

Devil: devil-take-the-hindmost, an elimination race run as a continuous series of sprints in which, at given intervals of, say, six laps, the last man to cross the finishing line drops out. This goes on until there are only two riders left to contest the final sprint. The devil is a popular entertainment in Sixes but, unlike the *points race*, is not a world championship event.

Entraineur: *motor-pace* driver.

Finishing line: a 50mm black line centred in a 720mm white line marked radially across the end of the finishing straight.

Gauge line: this is black and 20mm wide, and is marked on the circumference of the track 20cm from its inside limit. It is so called because the length of the track is measured along the inner edge. Since it indicates the shortest distance around, it is also the line the pursuiter follows.

Hand-sling: the grasp of hands and swing of the arm by which the active partner in a *madison* relays his partner into the race.

Jam: a mainly American term for *chase*.

Keirin: sprint event on track in which a file of no more than eight riders takes pace from a single *derny* for so many laps, and then, having been given a flying start, races unpaced for the line. There is no set distance for the event, but on a small track it tends to cover six laps, with the derny driver swinging off a lap and a half before the line. On a larger track like Leicester (333.33m) it is usually over five laps with just the final lap unpaced. The keirin, which originated in Japan, was introduced into the world professional track championships at Besançon in 1990.

Kermesse: literally, a village fete or fair (Flemish, *kermis*). The name often applied to a Belgian or Dutch *criterium*.

Madison: prolonged relay race between two-man teams. So called because it was at Madison Square Gardens, New York, in 1899 that Sixes were first organised on a team rather than an individual basis, so as to give one rider a rest period while the other maintained the team's continuous presence on the track. The term now applies to specific sessions, some lasting as long as 90 minutes, when both riders are in action. One is in the race, attempting to gain a lap by breaking away from the front of the *peloton* and rejoining it from the rear, or counter-attacking to prevent an opponent from doing so. His team-mate, meanwhile, is riding on relief at a more leisurely pace, and usually further up the banking, until the moment, decided between themselves, when their roles are reversed, and he is relayed into the fray with a *hand-sling*. Madisons are the heart of the Six, since the race is basically decided on laps gained (but see also *points*), and are also staged separately as championship events.

Motor-pace: a race in which each rider cycles immediately behind a motor-bike (see *derny*) and take his pace from it. A typical six-day motor-pace will last 15–20 minutes or cover 15km.

Neutralised: term applied to certain spells when the riders continue to circle the track but no laps may be gained (e.g. during warm-ups or after crashes), and to riders allowed time out with medical or mechanical problems.

Omnium: contest at track meeting to determine the best all-round performers. It may be for individuals or teams, and is made up of a medley of events, e.g. *pursuit, madison, points race, motor-paced race*, etc.

Peloton: the main group of riders in a race, excluding breakaways and stragglers.

Points: these are awarded on a fixed scale to teams placed in the sprints, *devils* and other events which support the *madison*, and were originally used as tie-breakers when teams were level on laps. Increasingly, though, these points are being converted into laps with a one-lap bonus given for every 100 points scored.

Points race: both a supporting feature in the Six and a world championship event, introduced for amateurs in 1975, for professionals in 1980, and in the Olympic Games of 1984. Points are awarded to the first four riders to cross the *finishing line* every, say, five laps. Victory, however, depends on laps gained, and the points decide the event only when riders are on the same lap.

Potato chase: a spell of *madison* racing during which the leaders allow the minor riders to gain easy laps, so making the contest appear closer than it is. At one time those who were not in serious contention for the overall lead identified themselves by sticking a potato under their saddles. That practice has stopped but the term remains.

Pursuit: championship event, for two individuals or two four-man teams, ridden by professionals over 5km, by amateurs over 4km and women over 3km. Opponents start simultaneously from opposite straights, and the winner is the first to complete the distance or to catch the other rider(s). In team pursuits the squads ride in single file, each man normally taking the lead for a half-lap or lap before swinging up the end banking and then dropping down to join the end of the file. The time of the third man to cross the finish is judged the time for the team.

Prime: literally, a prize. A bonus in cash or goods – now generally donated by a sponsor but in the past often put up by the public – for the first rider across the line after a given number of laps.

Sprinter's line: a red band, 50mm wide, marked around the track 90cm from the inside edge. In a sprint no rider may move below that line when a rider ahead of him is already on or inside it.

Soigneur: the rider's handler or second. Although he is principally a masseur, his work extends beyond that to medical care, supervision of diet, training advice and psychological support.

Stayer: a motor-pace rider – generally one who competes behind the big motors (see *derny*).

Stayers' line: a blue line, 50mm wide, which is marked around the track at one-third of its width from the inside edge. In motor-paced events the pacer and his rider must stay inside (i.e. to the left of) this line except when overtaking.

Taxi-driver: experienced six-day rider who is given the job of partnering a novice or a roadman who may be an accomplished in his own milieu but is unused to racing on the boards. In doing this he probably sacrifices his own chance of winning the race.

Bibliography

Frederick Alderson, *Bicycling, A History*
(David & Charles, Newton Abbot, 1972)

Roger De Maertelaere, *Zesdaagsen/Six Jours/Sechstagerennen*
(Uitgeverij Worldstrips, Ghent, 1991)

J. Durry, ed. J. B. Wadley, *The Guinness Guide to Bicycling*
(Guinness Superlatives, London, 1977)

Peter Nye, *Hearts of Lions: The History of American Bicycle Racing*
(WW Norton & Co, New York/London, 1988)

Andrew Ritchie, *The King of the Road, An Illustrated History of Cycling*
(Wildwood House, London, 1975)

Andrew Ritchie, *Major Taylor: The Extraordinary Career of a Champion Bicycle Racer* (Bicycle Books, San Francisco, 1988)

Charles Ruys, *Spotlight on 6 Day Races*
(Charles Ruys, England, 1967)

Roderick Watson and Martin Gray, *The Penguin Book of the Bicycle*
(Allen Lane, London, 1978)

Frank Westell and Ken Evans, *Cycle Racing*
New Edition (Springfield Books, Huddersfield, 1991)